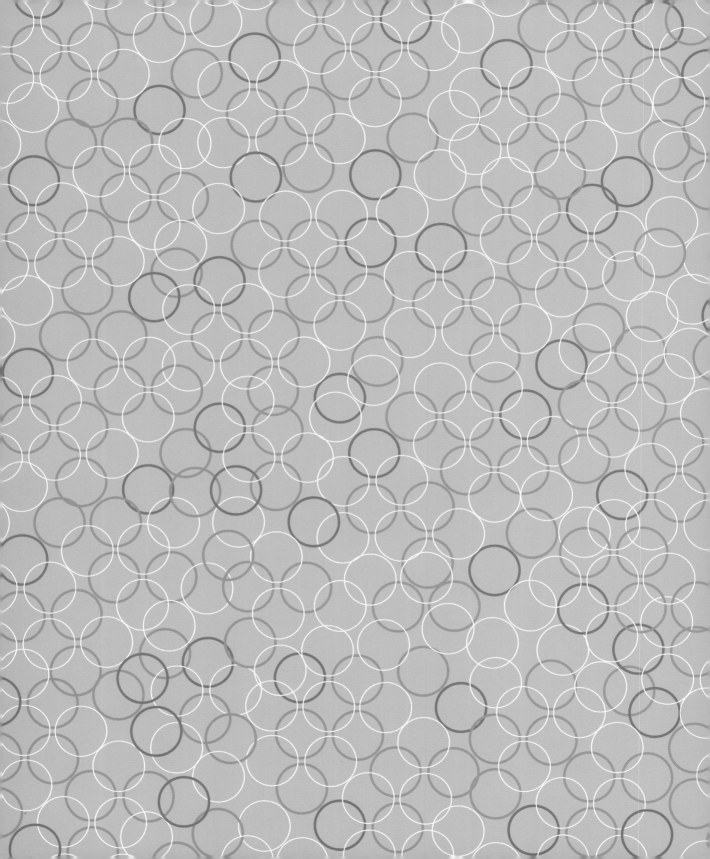

DONNIE BROWN WEDDINGS

from the couture to the cake

DONNIE BROWN

STEWART, TABORI & CHANG ⌒ NEW YORK

This book is dedicated to my partner, Matthew Lindley, for the many years of constant support and encouragement he has given me. I would not be the person I am today without him and am so very thankful and blessed to have him in my life.

CONTENTS

INTRODUCTION

The wedding day, for most people, is one of the most stressful days of their lives. I have a secret weapon. I try to use humor on a daily basis. Humor makes the day more fun and minimizes the stress on my important clients.

After years of being on the hit television show *Whose Wedding Is It Anyway?* on The Style Network, I have learned to master the art of grace under pressure—on camera! It is one thing to handle the day-to-day business of planning events, but it is another thing altogether to package these tasks as material for an entertaining television program.

I got my start in high school working part-time at a floral shop in Lubbock, Texas. In 1994, I ventured out on my own and opened Dallas-based Five Star Floral Design and Events. Soon I had established a reputation in town as a top-notch wedding professional.

In 2001, I had the good fortune of landing my first high-profile celebrity client. Country star LeAnn Rimes and her fiancé, Deane Sheremet, hired me to create the perfect look for their wedding. The couple was impressed by my enthusiasm and positive energy, which they knew I'd need for their star-studded nuptials. Since then, I've worked with other celebrities, including actresses Dixie Carter and Emma Thompson, and Sanya Richards, an Olympic Gold Medalist who holds the world record as the fastest woman in the world, and her fiancé, Aaron Ross of the New York Giants. I've planned parties for everyone from the Democratic National Committee to the Dallas Cowboys.

In 2003, I made my television debut on *Whose Wedding Is It Anyway?* After six seasons, I was shocked to find out that I had emerged as the fan favorite! When Style launched another wedding-related series in 2006, *Married Away*, I was asked to join that cast as well to help couples plan their destination weddings. Between tapings, weddings, and overseeing my event planning business in Dallas, I travel the country speaking at bridal expos and other wedding-related events. I always try not to disappoint. I generally do a part comedy routine, part informational talk on the value of hiring a wedding planner. Drawing on my professional experiences, I instruct couples on how to get through their big day.

Writing this book seemed to be the natural next step. There are so many couples who contact me to plan their weddings. The demand is simply too high for me to accommodate even a fraction of the requests. Within the following pages, I've shared how to create a Donnie Brown–style wedding, from the most simple of events to incredibly elaborate ones. My perspective on common planning conundrums, insight on figuring out wedding-day logistics, and the practices I use on a daily basis are all here.

Today's wedding couples and their families are striving to keep up with an ever-growing and advancing industry that has moved efficiently into the twenty-first century. The number of options the modern bride confronts while planning a wedding can be daunting. In reading this book, you will learn what to look for, what to ask, and how to manage the details of a wedding in a concise, efficient manner. After all, wedding planning is all about the details and the other details, and then even more details. I have also included a few entertaining stories from real weddings that are relevant to the topic at hand, as well as other tidbits of germane advice. Your wedding should be as close to your vision as possible—after all, you have been dreaming of it for years. This guide will help you achieve this dream. Keep a copy with you and refer to it as you maneuver through the jungle we call the modern wedding industry.

— Donnie Brown

PLANNING TIMELINE

When should it be done and who should do it? These are important questions that all brides and grooms ask themselves early on. Obviously this is not a hard-and-fast timeline, but rather a general timetable to help you organize.

10 to 12 months before

- ☐ Create a binder with ideas and wish lists.
- ☐ Research planners and schedule consultations. Hire your planner.
- ☐ Create a budget (at least establish a hard number of available funds).
- ☐ Pick a date, select a venue, agree on a maximum guest count. (These are together because often the guest count dictates the venue; the availability of the venue determines the date, and so forth.)
- ☐ Take engagement photos, which can be used for save-the-dates.

9 months before

- ☐ Buy a wedding gown.
- ☐ Select your wedding party.
- ☐ Begin compiling a guest list.
- ☐ Research and hire a photographer and videographer.
- ☐ Finalize contracts with ceremony and reception sites.
- ☐ Book vendors:
    Hire a caterer, if one is necessary.
    Hire entertainment.
    Hire a florist and/or décor specialist.

7 to 8 months before

- ☐ Make certain your passports are in order or apply for them.
- ☐ Order save-the-date cards and wedding invitations.
- ☐ Order the wedding cake.
- ☐ Begin creating a playlist for the ceremony and reception.
- ☐ Select attendants' attire.
- ☐ Sign up for a wedding registry.
- ☐ Secure hair and makeup stylists for the wedding day. Plan to do a dry run.

5 to 6 months before

- ☐ Book your honeymoon travel and accommodations.
- ☐ Book hotel accommodations for the wedding night.
- ☐ Finalize your guest list.
- ☐ Mail save-the-date cards.
- ☐ Finalize your menus.
- ☐ Hold fittings for bridal party.
- ☐ Hold first fitting for bridal gown, if it has arrived.
- ☐ Shop for wedding rings.

3 to 4 months before

- ☐ Groom selects tuxedo for wedding.
- ☐ Make sure all men have been measured for tuxedos and information has been submitted to the rental company.
- ☐ Mail wedding invitations.
- ☐ Book your wedding transportation.
- ☐ Shop for wedding accessories and jewelry.
- ☐ Finalize a playlist with the band or DJ.
- ☐ Reserve venues for pre-wedding festivities (bachelorette party, rehearsal dinner, etc.).
- ☐ Arrange sitters to look after your kids, pets, and/or house while you enjoy your honeymoon.

1 to 2 months before

- ☐ Final fitting of gown.
- ☐ Bridal portrait.
- ☐ Finalize wedding vows and/or ceremony.
- ☐ Hire valet if needed.
- ☐ Walk through reception site with vendors, if necessary.
- ☐ Hire an assistant to run errands and handle details on the wedding day, if you did not hire a planner.
- ☐ Notify insurance agents of changes to policies post-marriage.
- ☐ Purchase wedding event insurance.

3 to 4 weeks before

- ☐ Mail out rehearsal dinner invitations.
- ☐ Get marriage license.
- ☐ Make sure wedding party has all accessories and clothing needed.
- ☐ If moving to a new residence, call utilities and movers to arrange the move.
- ☐ Buy gifts for special people such as your mom, dad, spouse, and wedding party.
- ☐ Give place cards or escort cards to calligrapher.
- ☐ Finalize loose ends with your vendors, performers, or venues.

2 weeks before

- ☐ Call any guests who have not RSVP'd and give final head count to caterer or venue.
- ☐ Give final seating chart to caterer or catering director of the venue.
- ☐ Create a timeline for the wedding day and give it to parents, wedding party, and the officiant.
- ☐ Review all contracts.
- ☐ Confirm all reservations for hotels, restaurants, transportation, and honeymoon.
- ☐ Call all vendors and performers to confirm arrival and departure times.

1 week before

- ☐ Bride picks up dress.
- ☐ Groom picks up tuxedo.
- ☐ Make sure transportation specialists have addresses, maps, and schedules.
- ☐ Finalize delivery of wedding cake.
- ☐ Pack for honeymoon. Do not forget travel documents.

the day before

- ☐ Finish packing.
- ☐ Manicure and pedicure for the bride and bridal party.
- ☐ Pre-function activity for bride and groom.
- ☐ Rehearsal and rehearsal dinner.
- ☐ Hand out wedding party gifts at rehearsal dinner.
- ☐ Prepare water and a snack for the car transporting you between the ceremony and reception.

your wedding day

- ☐ Get up early.
- ☐ Eat.
- ☐ Do your hair and makeup.
- ☐ Enjoy your family and friends.
- ☐ Relax.
- ☐ Get dressed.
- ☐ Begin your new life together.
- ☐ Have fun.

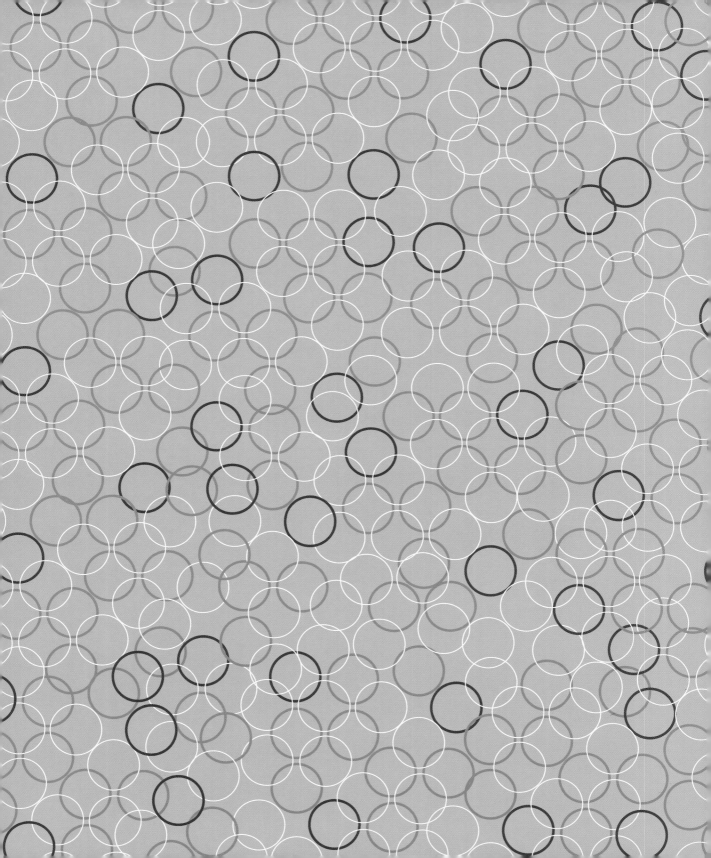

1

CHAPTER

GETTING STARTED

CHAPTER ONE *getting started*

You've just gotten engaged. Congratulations! You've dreamed of this moment and patiently waited for the proposal. Enjoy the roses and sunshine. The excitement is overwhelming, the air smells sweeter, the future is brighter. But now that you've got the ring, where do you start? Once you've adjusted to the newness of the situation, you'll need to get down to business and begin deciding what type of wedding you and your lucky groom want.

WHEN'S THE WEDDING?

This is the first question many people ask as soon as they hear someone is engaged, and, for most couples, it is not an easy one to answer. There is a great deal of research to be done prior to establishing the date.

HOW MANY PEOPLE SHOULD I INVITE?

You might want a small and intimate wedding, but just wait until your family and future in-laws get involved. They are probably going to provide you with lists of people, many of whom you have not seen since you were a child and some names you may never have heard of. A wedding is not just the beginning of a marriage, but also one of the most important networking events of one's life. You will find out quickly how important it is to all the people around you once you announce your engagement. Many of us never realize how many significant people are in our lives until we start jotting down a list. Once the tallying begins, it usually becomes a source of concern.

WHAT IS MY BUDGET?

You might think you can move through the process with an open-ended budget and tack on one thing after another, but that is a recipe for financial disaster!

Do you want a destination wedding, a local wedding, a home wedding? The answers to these questions will affect how you structure your budget. You should also write down a list ranking which components of your wedding are most important to you. When it comes time to allocate money to the catering, the décor, the venue, etc., you should have your priorities in place and spend accordingly.

GETTING ORGANIZED

It is never too early to get organized and begin visualizing your special day. It may help talking to friends who have already been through the process. Looking at magazines will help you articulate your likes and dislikes. You might also want to watch wedding-themed movies and reality wedding shows to get your creativity going.

A large notebook with dividers is the perfect way to organize your notes, magazine clippings, and photos into an easily accessible and mobile collection of ideas. Each divided section should represent an area of the wedding you need to plan or execute—the gown, the catering, flowers and décor, event design, photography—the list goes on. As you move through the planning process, this binder will also hold your contracts from the beginning stages, all the revisions, through the final draft. Once you begin to explore an area, such as dresses, remove or rotate rejected concepts to the back and move your current favorites and final decisions to the front. This will reduce the amount of searching you have to do each time you look for a particular train or bodice and will later represent how far you have come. Save space in the front for a calendar of vendor payments. Most vendor agreements and contracts will have stiff penalties for late or non-payment, not the least horrifying of which could be cancellation of your wedding contract without reimbursement of the monies already paid.

It's a good idea to allocate a bag or satchel as your wedding tote. Here you might include your wedding planning book, a good street map (if you need one to get around to all the different new locations you will be visiting during the planning process), bottled waters, pens and pencils, your keys, your phone, and even your purse. It is important to be punctual to your meetings, and having one bag with all the things you need will make arriving on time a little easier.

With your wedding tote in hand and many hours of daydreaming logged, the next step is to determine if you should contract a wedding planner to help you execute your event. In my estimation, a wedding planner is a must. At the end of the next chapter, you will know definitively whether a planner is right for you.

your wedding notebook

The categories needed within a wedding planning binder are:

- Wedding planner information
- Budget and payment information
- Planning schedule/logistics
- Guest list
- Ceremony venue
- Reception venue
- Floor plans/logistics
- Cake designs
- Gowns
- Attendants' attire
- Tuxedos
- Ceremony entertainment
- Reception entertainment
- Flowers/décor/lighting
- Rentals
- Photography
- Videography
- Invitations
- Save-the-date cards
- Programs/maps/menu cards
- Reception catering/menus
- Rehearsal
- Rehearsal dinner
- Transportation
- Hair/makeup
- Television/magazine coverage
- Pre-wedding events for him
- Pre-wedding events for her
- Engagement party
- Accommodations
- Guest travel
- Honeymoon
- Timelines
- Bride's family issues
- Groom's family issues
- Miscellaneous

Note: You may not need dividers for all of these. This is a comprehensive list, so use only those items that pertain to you and your event.

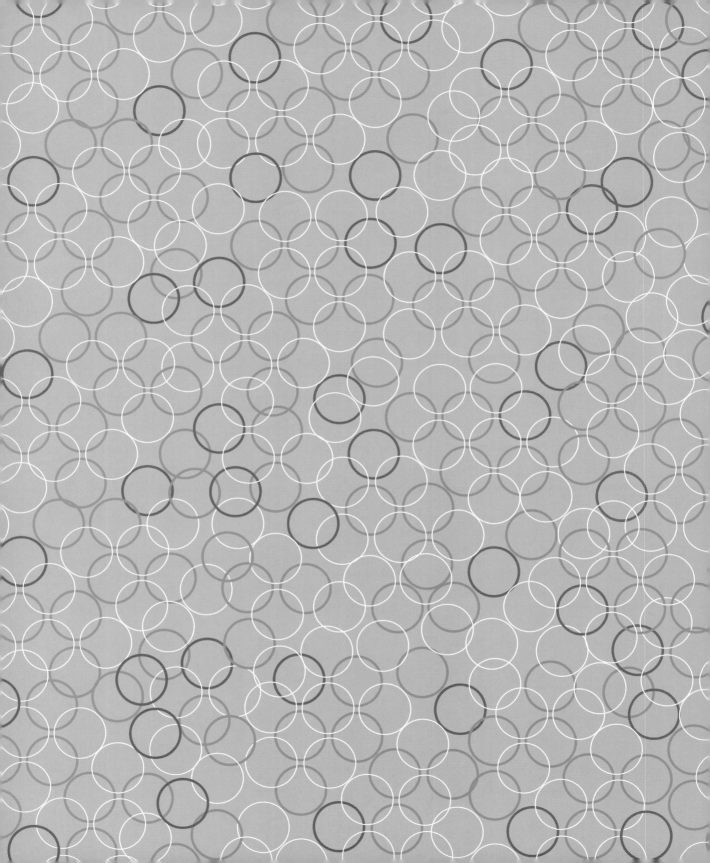

2

CHAPTER
SHOULD I HIRE A WEDDING PLANNER?

CHAPTER TWO *should I hire a wedding planner?*

Clearly, my opinion of wedding planners is extremely high—as long as they are certified by an accredited association and are good at what they do. I have the greatest respect for planners who have a well-established network of fine professionals in their inner circle.

THE WEDDING PLANNER'S ROLE

Do you have to hire a wedding planner to ensure a beautiful wedding? No, clearly you do not. However, a wedding planner can certainly make your life easier. In most cases, they have already researched your local wedding vendors and the multitude of potential venues. A good planner can save you untold hours—and most often money— by steering you away from unethical vendors and saving you from hidden charges. They will know up-front which days of the week carry the highest price tags and the best tactics for navigating through peak and off seasons.

How are you supposed to know the language used to book a reception area? If you want a buffet but also want everyone to have a seat in the dining area, do you know to say you want "capacity seating"? I recently had a bride who wanted seats for every guest, but the catering manager at a hotel misunderstood and thought she wanted "cocktail seating," which would only provide a place for around 50–70 percent of her guest list. This type of miscommunication ruins events. Having a professional walk you through the contracts and negotiations can eliminate such unwelcome surprises.

Wedding-planning challenges can arouse an incredible amount of emotion and distress, and the bride who wishes to achieve the perfect wedding day must overcome these obstacles. That is where a wedding planner comes in. A planner's principal responsibility is to educate and assist the bride, so that together they can create her dream wedding within the confines of a budget and without too many headaches.

FINDING THE ONE

To generate your preliminary list, speak to friends and family about planners they have hired for their previous events.

As with every profession, there are the good and the bad, so references from people whose opinions you respect are a great starting point. Additionally, refer to local wedding magazines and catalog the names of planners whose advertisements appeal to you and your personal style. An ad can tell you a lot about the planner. If the ad catches your eye, there is a good chance that you share a similar aesthetic. Although it's never a sure bet, it can be an effective method of screening. Once you have at least two strong candidates, set up appointments for consultation. If you are not the only decision maker in the planning process, make every attempt to include the others in these meetings. Good wedding planners and professional wedding vendors are busy with their lists of clients and often do not have time to do multiple initial appointments. Don't try to schedule one appointment to meet a planner, another to include your mother, and yet another with you and your fiancé. If you are wary of setting up these appointments without learning a bit more about the planners, look at their Web sites, request package information, or ask pointed questions over the phone. Don't be surprised if you get the feeling that you are being interviewed as well. Planners must weed out those people who are not a good fit for their company.

HIRE YOUR PERFECT MATCH

I strongly encourage meeting with several wedding planners before deciding not to use one. You may find you can be well served by their assistance: The fee to hire a wedding planner is often offset by his or her ability to negotiate deals with vendors, budget for unforeseen costs, and avoid sneaky hidden charges.

Make your decision wisely, because you will spend more time with your planner than anyone else. Hire someone with a personality that is compatible with your own. Your wedding planner will not only begin to feel like your best friend but at times will seem to be your only friend. Give the job to someone you'd enjoy shopping and having dinner with, because likely you will be doing a fair amount of both over the course of several months. Obviously, planners can only execute ideas that they understand. If you get the feeling the person you are meeting with doesn't comprehend, isn't willing to listen, or is constantly trying to change your overall concept, perhaps he or she is not the right planner for you and your wedding. Do not get discouraged if you meet with several before really clicking with someone. It's part of the process—one that will get infinitely easier and more enjoyable as you move along. Once a planner is hired, meetings with vendors will not be as daunting, because, regardless of whether you include your planner in all upcoming appointments, he or she can still brief you before each one.

be prepared

Before calling a wedding planner for a consultation, prepare answers for the following questions:

• What is your budget?
• How many guests are you estimating will attend?
• When is your event?
• Are you considering multiple events in addition to the ceremony and reception, such as welcome parties, bachelor and bachelorette events, bridal luncheons or teas, pre- or post-wedding brunches, or engagement parties?
• What items have you secured at this time?
• Are you the guarantor of the event or are there others, such as your parents, who will be footing the bill?

QUESTIONS TO ASK

How long have you been a wedding planner?

I would be reluctant to hire anyone with less than two years of full-time experience. It is a complicated business.

Do you plan weddings and events on a full- or part-time basis?

It is difficult to plan weddings part time. Many of the appointments will be during business hours. Further, you need to be able to reach your planner in a crisis situation, which can be difficult if they work another job.

If you are a part-time planner, what is your other job?

If the answer is plumber, perhaps this is not the planner for you. If the answer is working in a bridal boutique, this likely is a person whose entire professional life is the wedding business. Often new planners position themselves in the market to meet new brides as clients, with the understanding from their employer that this is one thing they will be doing. Working in a bridal shop or boutique is one way to generate new business leads. However, once these boutique associates/part-time planners develop a name for themselves, they wind up not being able to take care of their contracted clients as well as they would like and typically move on to planning full-time.

How many weddings do you plan in a year? In a month?

Each planner is different. Some handle one wedding per month and do not use assistants; others have assistants to help and handle multiple events in one weekend. Talk with prospective planners about how responsive they are to phone messages and e-mails. This will help you to understand in advance whether they really have time for you and your event. In my company, I oversee each wedding but assign planners from my staff to manage them. This arrangement allows me to take on more clients, and each bride feels she is being cared for daily, all the while having the assurance that I am in charge of her event. This has taken time to perfect, but it works very well.

Do you have any formal training? Are you a member of any associations? Are you certified?

There are several accredited wedding education institutions and associations. Formal training and education should be a must when making your selection. This is one of the most important days of your life and trusting it to an amateur could be one of the biggest mistakes you make. Associations cultivate relationships in the community and the industry. Vendors who are part of large wedding associations, such as June Wedding Inc., spend time working with each other, exchanging ideas, and understanding how the others work. Additionally, associations are discriminating when they admit their members and are not likely to tolerate unscrupulous or unethical behavior. Checking the Better Business Bureau for information on a planner or a wedding vendor is always a good idea. Many associations have continuing education programs to certify their members in different fields within the industry. The more established and comprehensive programs come from June Wedding Inc. (JWI), Association of Bridal Consultants (ABC), International Special Event Society (ISES), Association of Wedding Planners (AWP), and National Association of Catering Executives (NACE).

What happens if you are ill or cannot coordinate the wedding?

Make certain your contract clearly articulates the backup plan for illness, or a release from the contract in the event the planner is unable to execute the required duties. If your planner is pregnant, a clause dictating the operating procedure in the event of complications or early delivery is essential. Often called a "non-performance clause," this is a critical feature in any contract. Again, if your planner has assistants who are well aware of the details of your wedding, you have nothing to worry about. A professional wedding planner plans in advance for all possibilities.

What is the average wedding budget with which you customarily work?

If the answer is $1 million and you are planning to spend $40,000, perhaps you should keep looking. A huge disparity between the company's average and your budget might create problems. Planners accustomed to flying to New York to hire a couture designer who handcrafts gowns won't be as enthusiastic about working with the strip mall bridal boutique where you are selecting a gown off the rack.

What is your fee?

Consider the amount of time the planner will spend on your wedding and the specific ways he or she could save you money throughout the process. Then, plug this information into your budget to analyze the net effect of the expense. You may find after careful consideration that you are saving enough money to make the actual out-of-pocket expense negligible.

NEGOTIATING THE DEAL

Once you hire a planner you'll need to select from the company's packages, price brackets, and billing options.

Some planners require a percentage of the overall budget, as this is generally a good indicator of the amount of time, work, planning, and staffing the wedding will require. You should go to your consultation with a potential coordinator having a good idea of how hands-on you want the planner to be with regardw to your event. Do you want him or her to attend each and every meeting with you? Will you rely not only on the planner's expertise but also on his or her opinions to conceptualize the event? You are looking for a package that will fit your expectations of the planner's duties. Keep in mind that your planner will be steering you in the right direction with vendors and venues based on your budget, personality, and personal preferences, so in most cases the planner need not attend every meeting. Packages that require planners to attend every meeting are quite time-consuming and, therefore, expensive. Planners tend to have packages with a variety of price options. Some might bill by the hour, and based on the education and experience of that planner, this hourly rate can range from $25 to $250. A good rule of thumb is that a more expensive coordinator will do a job that is more complicated and with greater expertise than one who is inexpensive. It is often fair to assume that you'll get what you pay for.

You might also find a "day of" or "week of" planning package. With this option, a planner steps in and helps you finalize your event after the planning is nearly complete. Hiring someone to manage the event allows the bride and those closest to her to relax and enjoy the day.

It may be possible to customize a package based on your particular needs. If budget is an issue, you might book a lower-priced package and add some necessary à la carte items. This way you can avoid committing to a more expensive plan that contains services you don't need. Be realistic and make certain every service you require is included. As with any contract, do not expect verbal agreements or casually mentioned preferences to be contractual. Make a habit of following up any and all verbal communication with e-mail or fax to make sure there is a written summary of the conversation. This will assist you and the planner or vendor in making sure that no issue falls through the cracks. For e-mail, always set your program to ask the recipient for a read receipt so you know it has been received; this will act as your confirmation.

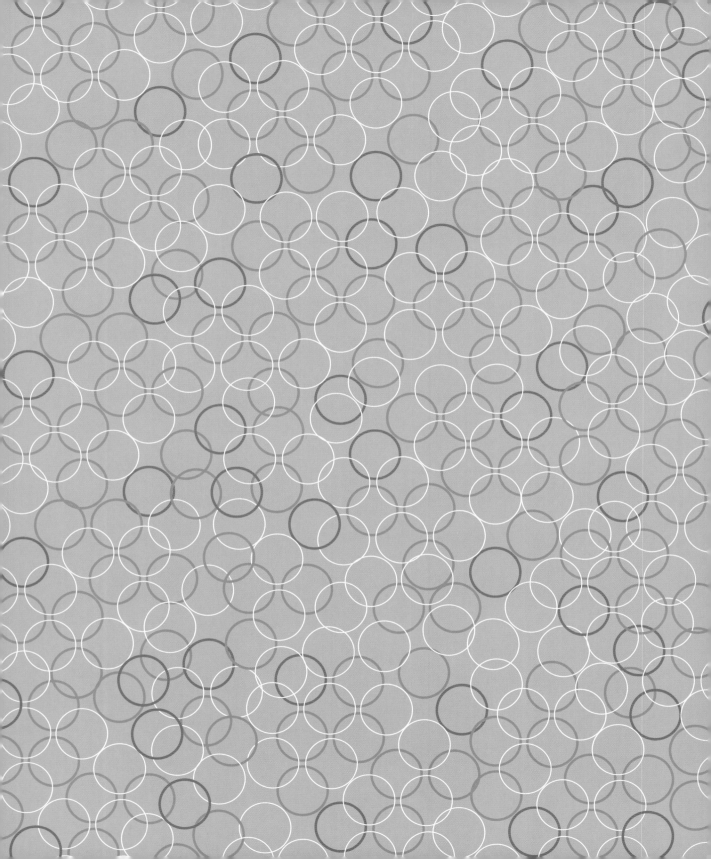

3

CHAPTER
BUDGET

CHAPTER THREE *budget*

Often, couples and their families develop their budget backward. They decide on each item individually and then move on to the next thing. This is a recipe for financial ruin. As myriad factors determine the breakdown of the budget, a dollar figure must be established. You need to determine who is contributing what and earmark a figure.

You should determine what you want to spend on the whole wedding and then break it down into each individual category. This eliminates getting caught with no money halfway through the process. Brides often rush out to purchase a gown and perhaps hire the photographer, and spend half of their budget before they get to the big-ticket items such as catering, décor, and entertainment. Research what is a good per-person budget for the type of wedding you want, multiply this by the number of guests, and then add 10–15 percent to that figure, and you should be close to the total cost of your wedding.

Be sure that you understand what a wedding in your area typically costs. Obviously, it is more expensive to hold a wedding in New York City than it is in Lubbock, Texas. People make different wages for the same work and pay different amounts for the same thing. Prices can even vary within neighborhoods of the same city. Take this into account when you are making decisions about budget and event location.

ORGANIZE YOUR FUNDS

The easier it is to access the money you have designated for your wedding, the smaller the chance of losing a treasured vendor while shifting money from mutual funds or saving accounts. Consider signing up for a credit card that offers travel or reward points. With every dollar you spend on your wedding, you could be earning miles toward a free first-class round-trip ticket to the destination of your choice. Expenses such as hotel rooms, the wedding gown, and car rental fees can all be paid for with this card. If you choose this option, pay the balance on the card monthly so you can enjoy the rewards without paying interest. If parents are contributing or paying for the event, have them make payments to the credit card directly.

Some vendors still do not accept credit cards, so there may be occasions when it is necessary to write a check. In these instances, having a checking account used solely for your wedding expenses will save you a tremendous amount of inconvenience.

In either case, it's a smart idea to use a credit card or checking account that has been established as a dedicated source for wedding funds. It is the best way to keep your accounting record organized and easy to reconcile.

PLAN FOR THE UNEXPECTED

I tend to insist that 10 percent of the overall budget be put into a contingency line to serve as emergency money to draw upon later, if needed. It is impossible to plan for every small expense, and certainly new and exciting concepts are discovered along the way, so it is wise to have some wiggle room. Consider your contingency budget line a non-interest-bearing savings account. It won't grow, but it will certainly come in handy if you need it down the road.

SET PRIORITIES

Before attempting a detailed budget, I always ask brides to list their priorities. If a bride comes to me with a $50,000 budget, and the flowers and décor are most important to her, we will likely cut corners on other items to achieve the look she wants.

The vendors are broken down in the rest of the book, and each chapter has a series of questions to ask during the consultation process. Additionally, you should consider the following when looking at all vendors:

• Do they have only a few photographs that show their work at other weddings?

This likely means they have little experience and have not done many events. Don't let them use your event as a learning experience.

• Does the vendor have a Web site?

If your potential vendor does not have a Web presence, they probably are new to the business or have no vested interest in moving their business into the modern era. You really do want to work with vendors on the cutting edge, if at all possible.

• Is the vendor a member of the Better Business Bureau or a professional wedding association?

It is a red flag if none of your other vendors has heard of this vendor. In most cities, businesses within the wedding industry frequently work together and are familiar with each other's work. Your caterer can likely recommend a quality table and chair rental company; your florist probably knows of a talented wedding photographer. You can save yourself time and money by asking a trusted vendor for referrals.

be realistic

It never ceases to amaze me how many clients come in with a $20,000 budget and expect to get a full wedding and a reception with a seated dinner and open bar for four hundred guests. It is going to be very difficult to do this in a way that would satisfy most brides.

When money is tight, I always tell clients to reconsider their number of guests. Now, I don't think $20,000 is a small amount of money, but in the world of weddings, it is.

Considering that you need to allocate 35 percent of the total budget to food and beverage, $7,000 of that $20,000 ought to be spent on catering. Divide that figure by four hundred and you have $17.50 per person. You cannot eat dinner in a restaurant for that amount of money, unless you want to hold your reception at McDonald's. Perhaps the bride and groom could enter the reception on the kiddie slide. What fun! Just a bit of food for thought.

SAMPLE BUDGET

Below is a model to help you develop your own wedding budget. It is important to calculate percentages so that you know how much of the total you are spending on each category. The following percentages are simply guidelines and will vary depending on your priorities.

ITEM	BUDGETED EXPENSES		ACTUAL EXPENSES		DIFFERENCE ($)
Accessory items	$650	0.65%	$625	0.62%	(25)
Accommodations	$450	0.45%	$625	0.62%	175
Cake	$2,600	2.60%	$2,425	2.42%	(175)
Catering	$31,500	31.50%	$31,725	31.62%	225
Ceremony entertainment	$1,200	1.20%	$1,000	1.00%	(200)
Ceremony set-up fee	$1,200	1.20%	$1,200	1.20%	-
Favors	$800	0.80%	$752	0.75%	(48)
Flowers/décor	$19,000	19.00%	$18,922	18.86%	(78)
Gifts	$1,000	1.00%	$850	0.85%	(150)
Gown	$7,500	7.50%	$7,500	7.48%	-
Invitations/programs/printing	$1,400	1.40%	$1,450	1.45%	50
Makeup artistry	$600	0.60%	$600	0.60%	-
Photography	$5,500	5.50%	$5,500	5.48%	-
Reception entertainment	$6,000	6.00%	$6,000	5.98%	-
Transportation	$1,100	1.10%	$1,800	1.79%	700
Tuxedos/formal wear	$1,000	1.00%	$850	0.85%	(150)
Videography	$4,000	4.00%	$4,000	3.99%	-
Wedding planner fee	$14,500	14.50%	$14,500	14.45%	-
TOTAL BUDGET	**$100,000**	**100%**	**$100,324**	**100%**	**$324**

TEN COMMONLY OVERLOOKED COSTS

When laying out your budget, don't forget to factor in the following expenses.

1. Service charge and gratuity for catering food and beverage. This usually amounts to 20–22 percent over the food and beverage cost. You must also add tax for the pre-service charge.

2. Framing and matting of pre-wedding portraiture. This can be pricey.

3. Valet parking fees. Don't let your guests' last memory of your wedding be reaching into their pockets to find cash for the valet.

4. Gown and other formal wear alteration fees. There will be multiple fittings and each one comes with a cost. Ask the gown boutique in advance to estimate the total for alterations fees and factor this into your budget.

5. Cake-cutting fees. Many venues require that you use their in-house pastry chef to create your wedding cake(s). If you choose to use an outside vendor, expect a cutting fee of $2.50 to $7.50 per person. This charge covers plates, flatware, and labor costs. Some venues that don't have an in-house pastry chef may still charge a per-person fee for this service, although usually lower than that mentioned above.

6. Overtime fees. If the party was supposed to end at 11 PM but you keep it rolling into the wee hours of the morning, it will cost you. The band, the photographer and videographer, and any of the other vendors who plan on striking the event will all charge overtime fees if they end up working past the time initially agreed upon in their contracts.

7. Postage. Postage for invitations and response cards, which must all be stamped before you mail them.

8. Consumption vs. package bar. Consumption bars charge for every drink served. Package bars charge one upfront estimate.

9. Calligraphy. Everything about a wedding invitation should be perfect, including the penmanship on the envelopes. Don't use labels or personally handwrite the addresses yourself; hire a professional.

10. Wedding-day accessory items. Don't forget the guest book, pen, cake knife and server, ring bearer pillow—the list goes on. Personally, I like to buy these items in the beginning and incorporate them into the wedding's theme.

tipping your vendors

Tipping stumps many couples. There are no hard-and-fast rules. Caterers and hotel venues with in-house catering departments as well as most restaurants and clubs automatically add the gratuity to your final bill. If you ever see a tip jar on the bar at your wedding reception, remove it immediately. The bartenders are already sharing in the billable gratuities. Asking for additional tips is tacky.

As for the florist, the photographer or videographer, the band, the wedding planner, etc., how much you tip is your call. If a wedding professional puts forth no additional effort, they shouldn't expect a tip. For those who go the extra mile, an additional envelope of cash is absolutely acceptable. As for how much to put in that envelope, it is entirely up to you. Nobody goes to work at a wedding expecting a tip, but it is always appreciated.

PAYING VENDORS

As you begin booking venues and vendors, the one thing you can count on is a hefty deposit followed by multiple installments. Although every business structures its payment plan differently, the following are some industry standards:

Church venues: full payment due upon signing the contract.

Reception venues: at least 30 percent of the total food and beverage estimate and any rental fees due upon signing the contract; total balance due thirty days before the wedding.

Floral designers/decorators: 40–50 percent deposit; total balance due at least thirty days before the wedding.

Photographers/videographers: 30–40 percent deposit; total balance due at least thirty days before the wedding.

Bands/DJs: 50 percent deposit; total balance due sixty days before the wedding.

Wedding planners: 50 percent deposit upon booking; final payment due at the halfway point between signing the contract and the wedding date. (If your planner charges a percentage of the event's total cost and you exceed your estimated budget, you will owe a percentage of the difference thirty days before the wedding.)

Invitation designers, bridal gown boutiques, gown designers, tuxedo rentals, etc.: 50 percent deposit; total balance due upon arrival of order (even if there are future alterations necessary).

AMOUNT OF ESTIMATED CHARGES IN PENALTIES FOR CANCELING A RECEPTION VENUE

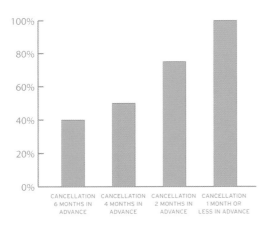

CANCELLATIONS AND DATE CHANGES

The best advice I can offer: Be certain about your date before you book.

Cancellations are usually met with stiff penalties. The less notice you give the venue, the more you'll have to pay. Some venues include a chart in their contracts outlining the increased amount you would owe as you move closer to your date (see sample, left).

Venues are typically more willing to accommodate a date change. However, even if you mutually agree to a new date, venues and vendors will rarely allow you to adjust your payment plan. Be prepared to continue with the one previously established.

4

THE VENUE

CHAPTER FOUR *the venue*

Selecting locations for the ceremony and reception is one of the most monumental decisions you will make in the wedding-planning process. Again, priorities come into play here. I often have a bride who insists on a particular date, which limits us to only those venues available that day. On the other hand, some brides insist on a particular venue, but never stop to think whether it can properly accommodate her three hundred guests. As a couple you will need to decide what is most important to you. The date? The guest list? The venue? The answer is different for everyone.

One of the first questions I pose to couples is, "Where do you see your wedding taking place?" Most often, this will guide us to that perfect location, or it will unearth some differences of opinions. If compromise has not been a big part of your relationship before, get ready to start practicing.

Typically, once we create a list of desired locations, a date or date range is generated based on the availability of potential venues. If the date is flexible, a savvy bride and groom can maximize their wedding budget by getting married off-season (generally between late December and March, depending on the climate), excluding holidays, or by considering any time other than a Saturday evening. It seems most of my brides are emotionally attached to Saturday evenings in the spring or early summer months, as well as winters in warm, sunny places, all of which carry a premium price tag. Keep in mind that most guests can find the time to attend a ceremony on any day of the year if it is a priority. Friday, Saturday morning or afternoon, and Sunday weddings are growing more popular because minimum food and beverage requirements and minimum packages with vendors are often much lower.

Ceremonies held outside of a church are ideal for this option, but churches have less availability for non-Saturday-evening ceremonies due to Mass schedules or other internal activities.

SITE SCOUTING

As a sacred part of the wedding, the ceremony's location will depend on religious affiliation, personal and family preference, and convenience to the couple, their families, and guests. The venue selected for the reception will likely be based on capacity, food and beverage minimums, visual appeal, space size, convenience to guests, and personal preference. It is becoming increasingly popular to hold the ceremony at the same location as the reception. Often, due to the amounts of money spent on receptions, a hotel or event center will offer an attractive unused space for the ceremony for a small set-up fee, which is generally much less than the cost of holding a wedding at a church, chapel, or synagogue.

While researching venues, consider your interactions with the people selling the space. Does the venue's staff seem open to making the venue work for your wedding, or are they more interested in making your wedding fit their space? Do they sound knowledgeable about the questions you are asking? Do they respond in a timely fashion to your messages? You want a venue that is willing to accommodate your event. However, you must also keep in mind that wedding vendors and venue sales managers do not work banker's hours. They generally work late on weekend nights and are often not in the office on Mondays or early mornings, so don't hold it against them if they do not answer your call at 8 AM on Monday. If it is a desirable site, they are probably fielding a lot of calls from other potential clients as well; multiple calls may slow down the response time even further.

When looking into venues for your ceremony or reception, make sure to do a site inspection prior to booking, if at all possible. You want to ensure you are completely happy with the space, décor, and staff. A site inspection may also influence your decisions when selecting a caterer (if there is not one in-house), a floral designer/decorator, or the entertainment. Look closely at the size of the space to ensure it will easily accommodate the size of your wedding guest list. Make sure you like the lighting, the chairs, the table sizes, the china, silverware, and glassware. If you are not able to personally visit the site, ask the venue's sales manager to send you photos of everything you want to see, including the room when it is empty, the items offered, and some sample images of the venue when it is decorated for other weddings.

A CHURCH CEREMONY

If you book a church for your ceremony, there are several factors beyond availability to consider. Capacity is generally not an issue, unless you have selected a quaint chapel, but often a large sanctuary can be a bit overwhelming for a small ceremony. Church rules are normally extensive and put in place to preserve the sacred environment. Count on regulations regarding décor, and don't be surprised if you are required to donate any flowers used during the ceremony to the church. Some religions provide couples counseling or retreats prior to the ceremony and some still will not perform interfaith weddings. Before deciding on a church, look at the sanctuary carefully. A chief structural consideration is the width of the center aisle. There must be ample room for you and your escort to walk without fear of interfering with décor or having your dress stepped on.

Consider carefully the rules regarding photography. Most churches will not allow flash photography during the ceremony and will only allow photographers to shoot from the balcony or back of the church. As for videography, some will not allow an unmanned camera on the altar. Many couples want a photo of the ring exchange. This might not happen if rules forbid positioning a camera on the altar. Consider all the images you want from your ceremony and read between the lines when reviewing the restrictions outlined in your contract.

the logistics

The time of your ceremony will dictate the flow of your wedding day. Typically you will need to reserve a time slot, which is necessary since most churches only hold three to four ceremonies per Saturday. Regardless of which time slot you book, be sure to allocate time for arrival, dressing, dispersal of flowers, pre-ceremony photos, the entire length of the ceremony, post-ceremony photos, and time to clean the facility prior to leaving the premises.

If you want to include your ceremony flowers in the post-ceremony photography and then transfer them to the reception, you should note that it is bad form to move floral arrangements or décor in front of your guests. After everyone has left the service, the floral design or décor team will need adequate time to remove the flowers and/or décor from the church, transfer it to the reception, and place it before the guests' arrival. Carefully outline the timing and logistics with your florist well in advance. A simple solution is to have a cocktail hour in a space separate from the reception room. This way the décor staff will have ample time to set up the reception space before your guests are seated.

A church ceremony offers a lovely, meaningful experience for you and your family. However, if you decide to not hold your ceremony in a church due to the long list of rules, you wouldn't be the first.

A CHURCH SOCIAL HALL RECEPTION

For those couples who do not require an elaborate party or prefer not to offer alcohol for a variety of personal reasons or budgetary constraints, the church's social hall is a perfect location for a coffee, punch, and cake reception. An important note here is that a coffee, punch, and cake reception lends itself nicely to a morning ceremony and offers a budget-friendly alternative to hosting an evening event. Although some halls may be spacious enough for large groups to dance and mingle, some social areas double as Sunday schools, daycare centers, or disaster shelters. Before committing to a social hall, a site check is imperative.

Considerations when deciding on a church social hall include: Does the venue offer tables, chairs, linens, china, glassware, silverware, etc.? Will there be a crew there to assist in the setup and cleanup of the event? Who will cut and serve the cake? The money you think you'll save by having an event in this space will quickly be spent if you have to rent items not available at the church.

A HOTEL CEREMONY

It didn't take long for hoteliers to catch on to the incredible income potential of having a lovely event space. In the past few decades, hotels have become a preferred wedding venue. An increasing number of brides are also solving their logistical dilemmas by having their ceremony and reception at the same location.

Given that the bulk of your wedding budget will be spent on the reception, it is entirely likely that a generous hotel will offer additional unused space for a ceremony. These spaces come in the form of garden rooms, gardens, smaller event sites or ballrooms, boardrooms, or even palatial suites with balconies. You can even use the same room for the ceremony and the reception if you move your guests into the pre-function space outside the ballroom for a cocktail hour while the hotel staff turns the ballroom into the reception area. Of course, with all the above options, adequate space for a seated ceremony is a must—although I have done a few short, standing-room-only ceremonies and received few complaints. If you do opt for standing room only, you should have two to three rows of chairs in front so guests in the back of the room will have a better view.

There are many benefits to holding your wedding in a hotel. The staff, which is well trained in customer service, can easily set up a post-ceremony cocktail hour before the reception. This solves all travel, weather, floral transfer, and traffic issues between the ceremony and reception, which translates to fewer logistical problems and less opportunities for plans to go awry.

Hotels are also skilled in turning ceremony spaces into reception areas during cocktail hours. This must be carefully planned well in advance in order to carry out a seamless transformation. The last thing you want is a lengthy cocktail hour because it takes too long to redecorate the ceremony room for the reception. Discuss the timing with the venue's catering manager, the banquet manager, the floral designer, and anyone else involved in ensuring a timely room change. Don't leave anything to chance. Talk with your photographer in advance, and make sure he or she is given time to shoot the decorated reception space before guests are ushered in.

A HOTEL RECEPTION

Regardless of where your ceremony takes place, a hotel ballroom can be an excellent choice for your reception. The aesthetics are usually pleasing, there are plenty of additional power sources for entertainment and lighting effects, and adjacent rooms can often be used for a cocktail hour or perhaps even childcare.

Hotels readily offer special rates for room blocks, and your guests will undoubtedly appreciate the convenience of such suites. It is not uncommon for the rehearsal, rehearsal dinner, bridal luncheon, ceremony, reception, and a farewell brunch all to take place on the same property.

A hotel ballroom or event space is typically built in conjunction with a kitchen and has adequate service space in close proximity to the event. Accustomed to pampering their customers, hotels can generally provide a high guest-to-staff ratio, which results in a content, well-taken-care-of wedding party.

A GARDEN OR PUBLIC PARK

A garden or public area is an entity all its own. In your mind's eye you may see the perfect setting, but if it is city, county, or state property, permits will be required. If it is a public park or garden, you will want to contact the city hall. Check with the city clerk to find out which department handles these permits. Generally it is the parks department, but every city is different. Do this early so you don't miss your chance. As with any venue, it is first come, first served.

A public space is just that: public. So, you must plan for onlookers and pedestrian traffic, which could diminish the intimacy of the moment. If you are not shy and feel the more the merrier, then sally forth. I have visited countless public arenas that would make a glorious setting for a wedding, but holding a ceremony in a public or private space that was not built to hold events will pose certain issues that must be considered carefully, including guest seating, ceremony setup, and perhaps power for lighting and sound amplification.

If your dream is a privately owned public space, such as a conservatory or other managed area, you will need to rent it from the owners and follow their guidelines. If your fantasy is exchanging vows on a hilltop in the middle of nowhere, consider parking, the distance guests must walk, seating, and most of all, a backup plan for weather. The date will also need to be based on the climate in your region.

A PRIVATE CLUB

Country clubs, social clubs, supper clubs—the private club is ideally suited for a wedding ceremony and/or reception hosted by people who want to have an intimate home setting in a space large enough to accommodate their guests. Geared toward entertaining, these spaces are usually equipped with adequate power for lighting and entertainment and have plenty of space for cocktails, dinner, dancing, and even quiet areas for socializing.

If you are a member of a club, you are likely on semi-personal terms with the staff and will be able to communicate your desires, budget, and expectations. If you are a regular client, the staff may already be familiar with you and your family and be more inclined to accommodate you and your event.

In a country club setting, you are often afforded luxurious views of lush landscapes, which provide wonderful backdrops for photography and beautiful vistas for guests. A supper club or business club is generally set in an office building or tower, which often has a spectacular city skyline or seascape view. Consider the views at night. It often looks different than it does during the day. I'd suggest visiting the property at the same time of day that you've scheduled for your wedding, just to be sure it is exactly what you have in mind.

Generally, you must be a member to hold an event in a private club, or you may require a sponsor. However, some clubs open their facility to the public during wedding season for a nominal fee.

There are perks to having a wedding at a private club, such as wedding packages that include privileges at the club's golf course. Always weigh all the apples and oranges when making your decision.

A RENTAL FACILITY

A rental facility can be a mansion, an art gallery, a pavilion, a symphony hall, or any number of locations. Although many rental facilities offer a unique reception space, they also come with rental fees. Hotels, restaurants, and other venues that charge a food and beverage minimum tend not to add on an extra fee simply to use their space.

A PRIVATE RESIDENCE

A private residence can provide an intimate backdrop. Initially, people assume they will save a bundle by having the ceremony at home. However, there are considerable logistical issues to be aware of, most notably parking, seating rental, a tent as backup if the ceremony is to be held outside, bathroom facilities for a large group, and lighting for evening events.

In most cases, a private residence is not set up for large events, so count on having to rent almost everything necessary to provide dinner and entertainment for your guests. After receiving price quotes for renting napkins, silverware, china, crystal, serving utensils and appliances, chairs, chair covers if necessary, tables, a tent, lighting, additional required power, food, beverages, air conditioning or heating units, staff, and entertainment, couples learn quickly how expensive backyard weddings can become. (The caterer or floral designer can handle these rentals for you, should you decide on a home wedding.) You should also make sure that the caterer has adequate space for food preparation. And if you have a family pet, you ought to take into account guests with allergies.

Often, people also want to update or refurbish their home before hosting a wedding. If redecorating or construction is required, the expense should be factored into the wedding budget.

I have seen just about everything, and in my estimation, weddings held at a private residence, with or without a planner, have the greatest margin of error. From fire ants to tempestuous weather to accommodating handicapped guests to melting cakes, it requires tremendous know-how and limitless resources to implement a perfect homespun event.

A RESTAURANT

It's no secret that a restaurant is a great place to throw a party. Unlike many of the options listed in this chapter, a restaurant or food service venue will already have all the things you need: tables, chairs, dishware, an attached kitchen, public restrooms.

The thing to consider with a restaurant or bar is that in order for an establishment to close down for a night to hold your private event, it must charge a food and beverage minimum equal to the amount earned on a night with normal customers. If the business typically generates $15,000 in revenue on a Saturday night, the owner will expect you to guarantee this figure. Plus, you will have to purchase your alcohol from the restaurant (unless it's BYOB), which is always costly.

Beyond this, hosting a reception at a restaurant is relatively easy. The atmosphere is already established, the menu is easily assembled, and you won't have to fuss with a long list of rentals, if you are happy with the items they offer you. If you have a favorite restaurant, you may find that it is the perfect venue for your reception.

A CORPORATE SPACE

Architecture firms and other businesses have gorgeous facilities that they occasionally rent for private events. These spaces often feel more modern than ballrooms and country clubs. Some will require you to use a specific caterer, while others will allow you to use the catering company of your choice. Either way, count on the food having to be transported, and insist on references and a tasting.

A considerable drawback to these spaces is the increased security post–September 11. Most office buildings taller than four stories have elevated their security procedures and will not allow people to enter the building without specific safety measures and strict operating protocols. This causes a planning and execution nightmare for almost all vendors, who will likely be shuttled through loading docks and be subject to intense scrutiny upon entry, potentially causing delays.

Speaking of scrutiny, read contracts issued by these facilities very closely. You may come across a clause stating that your contract would be negated in the event that the building is sold or the contracted in-house caterer is fired. It is critically important that you understand the venue's cancellation policy. If, for whatever reason, they are unable to hold your wedding on their property, you need to know your legal rights. Check with an attorney and have the contract carefully read to make sure that you are covered.

PRICING AND FEES ASSOCIATED WITH WEDDING VENUES

Pricing and upfront fees can vary greatly. In most cases, you will encounter minimum food and beverage requirements. This means, in order to hold your event in this location, you will need to spend a certain amount of money on these items. This figure could be quoted as a minimum per-head charge or as a flat fee. While the average food and beverage cost is about $125 per person, it can range from $25 to thousands, depending on the fare, the location, the quality of liquor served, and whether the event has an open bar. (Keep in mind, this per-person charge will generally not include tax, gratuity, valet fees, or parking.)

For instance, let's say your venue's food and beverage minimum is $5,000. If you are hosting an event for one hundred guests and have selected a menu that costs $85 per head, you will have exceeded the minimum and will owe the overage, tax, gratuity, and general parking fees on top of this amount. The minimum is not necessarily how much you will spend; it is how much you must spend to hold your event at that venue. This system has been developed over the years to use in place of rental fees. Food and beverage minimums are generally nontransferable. If you are paying $35 a head for your one hundred guests and the venue has a minimum of $5,000, you probably won't be able to apply the balance to tax, gratuity, or parking. However, some venues will allow you to apply it to guest rooms, security, or facility-offered décor. Each venue is different—don't be afraid to ask or negotiate.

more questions to ask
during the site inspection

- **Will rented space be private from other guests in the establishment?** Many couples aren't comfortable with the possibility that the venue's other guests could interfere with their private event.
- **How closely are events booked together on the same day?**
- **What is your staff-to-guest ratio based on menu style and food and beverage service?**
- **What is your deposit and payment schedule?** A late or delinquent payment can result in termination of your contract, often leaving you scrambling to find a new venue. Also, remember that a venue won't hold your date unless they have a signed contract and deposit.
- **Do you take credit cards?** Companies that do not take credit cards tend to be less structurally sound. Consider this carefully when booking services.
- **What is your setup and strike (removal of setup) policy and timing for my event?** Vendors must have adequate time to do their jobs well.
- **Do you have in-house caterers? Can I hire my own caterer?** This is particularly important if you dislike the in-house caterer or wish to work with a specific caterer.
- **Do you offer private space for the bride and groom?** Newlyweds often welcome a little one-on-one time before the reception.
- **If a hotel, do you provide a bridal suite for dressing? If so, what is the charge?** High-end hotels may provide a space for you to use as a dressing room. Don't even think about using the honeymoon suite.
- **Do you have décor restrictions?** Look elsewhere if the venue won't allow you to create the wedding you want.

A DESTINATION WEDDING

Booking your wedding at an exotic destination is always a possibility. A destination wedding can offer romantic settings, great sightseeing, and a wonderful way for the two families to vacation together and become better acquainted. You don't have to travel thousands of miles away, either. You can have a beach wedding in many states within the United States, as well as in the Caribbean or Mexico.

The main thing to note is that you can actually save money by having a destination wedding because guest lists tend to be smaller. The extended family, business associates, and many friends that would have come had the wedding been nearby aren't as likely to buy a plane ticket to your exotic location. In fact, many couples decide to do a destination wedding to maintain control of the number of guests. Before making a final decision, consider the cost of travel for you and your guests, as well as how much you will miss those who may not be able to travel, such as elderly grandparents and expectant mothers.

In recent years, romance departments, which are essentially information bureaus on wedding planning, have been popping up at venues around the world—making it easier than ever to throw an event outside the United States. They handle weddings, honeymoons, and other social events, and can give you all the rules regarding marriage licenses and the laws of their country. The critical thing you must be prepared for is the cultural and communication differences that may arise when planning a wedding abroad.

A wedding planner who is well versed in destination weddings can certainly come in handy, effectively communicating your wishes to vendors and ensuring your needs are met. This does not mean you must fly your wedding planner to the destination in advance of the wedding or even for the event itself. They can make all of your wedding arrangements from afar so when you arrive at your wedding location, everything goes according to plan.

With a destination wedding, you are not required to pay for your guests' air travel or hotel accommodations. You may, however, want to work out a special price for their accommodations and, perhaps, group travel pricing with a specific airline or travel bureau. Check with your wedding planner or your romance department agent to find out whom you should contact to make these types of arrangements.

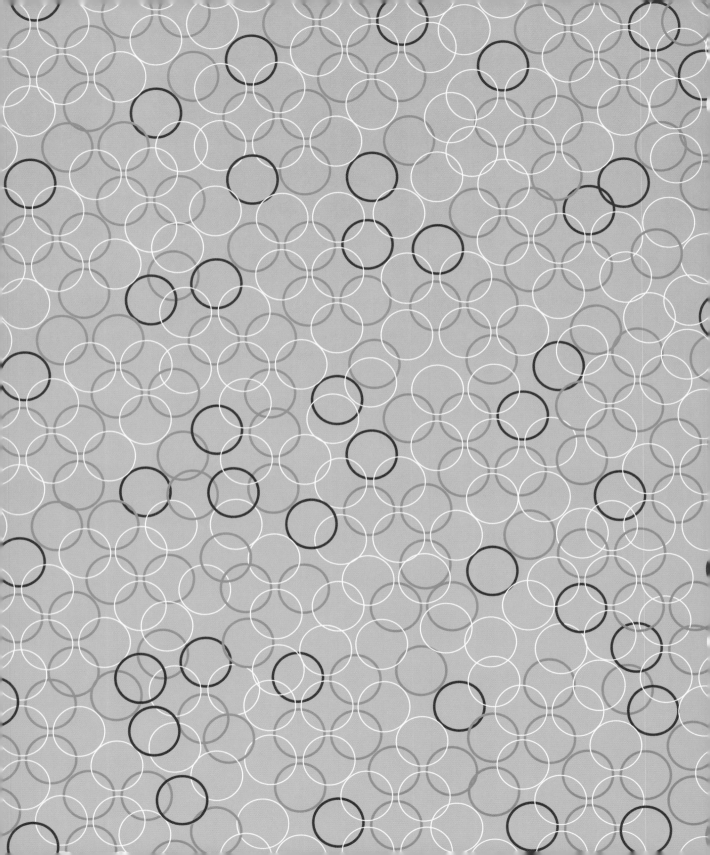

5 CHAPTER
THE
GUEST LIST

Guests

Names

Michael Blul

Randolf 1755

Wolf

CHAPTER FIVE *the guest list*

Few other aspects of the wedding will cause as much agitation as creating and inevitably whittling down your guest list. Without a doubt, the guest list will play a large role in the selection of an appropriate venue, or a desired venue will dictate the size of the list.

Either way, certain rules do apply. Generally speaking, the bride's family, if paying for the event, will invite the largest number of guests. Next or perhaps first, depending on how the family has decided to structure guest selection, will be the bride's and groom's lists, and finally, the groom's family's list. Be sure to consider the difference between the number of invitations and the number of guests allocated to each invitation. One invitation could translate to two or more guests. Many brides ask me if they have to put "and guest" on the invitation. Consider how you would feel if you were invited to a wedding but not allowed to bring anyone with you. Most people hate attending events alone and may even RSVP for a guest regardless, especially if they won't know many of the other guests attending. The exception to this rule would be the small, intimate family wedding.

Don't be shocked when everyone's list, including your own, is much larger than you expected. If you have created an overall budget, now is a good time to start itemizing. By now, you have looked at ceremony and reception sites and will have a good idea of the cost per head. If you have allocated $30,000 to your reception and you find all parties combined have developed a list of six hundred people, you might have to re-evaluate either the list or the venue. A $50-per-head rate might not be feasible at the venue you have your heart set on.

When you are working on your list, you will probably want to separate the guests into four categories—family, extended family, friends, and business associates. Prioritizing your long list of potential guests makes trimming it down much easier.

I have found the process goes more smoothly if the reception venue has already been booked. This way, if the space cannot accommodate more than one hundred people, there is no room for arguing. The bride and groom, or whoever is contributing the bulk of the financing, may dole out a number to each person and they will have to stay within those perimeters. You should understand that feelings will be hurt, so the more damage control you can do in advance the better. Start dropping hints about a finite number of guests and speak often about how hard it will be to make selections. Let family members know how torn you will feel; hopefully, they will limit the stress they place on you.

If your guest list is more important to you than where you hold your reception, this will be a relief to all, but there may still be some challenges. Weddings with guest counts above five hundred are difficult to place and will be expensive, regardless of the venue. Feeding so many guests will drive the price up, even if you select the least expensive menu options and a limited alcohol package.

Some brides and grooms opt to eliminate alcohol or create a cash bar to save money, but I find this to be rude. Guests have devoted their day to your wedding; a good many of them would enjoy a glass of wine. Without a few cocktails, many guests will never venture out onto to the dance floor, and you can count on a good many of them making an early departure. A cash bar is an antiquated notion and frowned upon in the wedding industry, but if you are determined to maximize your guest list, it is an option. However, in my opinion, a wedding is the one event in your life where a hosted bar is an absolute necessity. You can throw a party with a BYOB policy or a cash bar at any other time, but not at your wedding.

What if the bride's and groom's families live thousands of miles from each other? If the bride's family lives in Boston and the groom's lives in Seattle, it may make sense to hold the wedding and reception on the East Coast and then host a less formal second reception on the West Coast after the couple returns from their honeymoon. This is often a good solution for the bride and groom who are emotionally attached to a small, intimate venue with only immediate family and dearest friends.

The most important thing to remember is that every guest costs a certain dollar amount. For every person invited there is food, a chair, a percentage of a tablecloth and centerpiece, lighting, china rentals, a napkin, etc. The list goes on and on, based on the complexity of your event. Make these decisions wisely and don't panic when you start getting a lot of "yes" replies in the beginning. The yeses always come first and there will always be more "no" than "yes" RSVPs later on.

WEDDING GIFT REGISTRIES

You can register wherever and for whatever you want, but I strongly suggest registering only with stores that offer online shopping. Otherwise your out-of-town friends and family may find buying off your registry difficult. I generally suggest a minimum of three registries that include items with a wide range of prices. As a kindness to your guests, you should be sensitive to the fact that not everyone can afford to splurge on your gift. Another note is to make the registries versatile; you should not register at two bed and bath stores. Register at a bed and bath store, a department store, and perhaps a home improvement store. And keep in mind that most grooms don't get excited over china patterns, so include some items on the list for him as well.

How do I let my guests know where I am registered? I hear this question from almost everyone. The answer used to be that the bride's attendants should spread the word. In today's ever-changing electronic world, you have other options. Consider creating a wedding Web site. Among other information, this site can include your list of registries along with links to the appropriate Web sites. This simplifies the process so much and will keep you from getting six gravy boats from well-intentioned guests who have no clue what you need. A wedding Web site can be inexpensive, and some large wedding sites, such as The Knot, offer complementary Web sites simply for registering. You will also find that some wedding planners offer a custom-designed site to their clients.

A SHORT LIST OF POPULAR WEDDING REGISTRY SITES

- Tiffany and Company
  www.tiffany.com/registry
- Neiman Marcus
  registry.neimanmarcus.com
- Bed Bath and Beyond
  www.bedbathandbeyond.com
- Crate and Barrel
  www.crateandbarrel.com
- Home Depot
  www.homedepot.com
- Williams-Sonoma
  www.williams-sonoma.com/registry
- Target Club Wed
  www.target.com/registry/wedding/portal
- Macy's Wedding Channel
  www.macys.weddingchannel.com
- Pottery Barn
  www.potterybarn.com/registry

CHILDREN AS GUESTS

When you are developing your guest list, you should consider whether you want children to attend your wedding. Children can be a lot of fun and many people want to include them at family events. But along with the positives there are definite negatives. If you are holding a wedding with a band and an open bar, children should not be under foot. There are reasons why children are not allowed in bars. When people drink, they often lose their ability to consider how it affects kids. Then, there are the babies. Babies need sleep, peace, and constant attention. I usually ask parents to sit toward the back of the ceremony just in case they need to leave abruptly with a crying little one. The ceremony is one thing, but the reception is another. I cannot tell you how many people have brought small infants into loud wedding receptions filled with drinking and dancing. If you want to include your young nieces and nephews, arrange for a playroom at the reception and hire a couple of certified nannies.

If you decide not to invite children, I suggest putting "number of adults attending" on the RSVP card. This is a subtle way of saying that you are opposed to minors at your event. Whichever way you go, be sure to consider whether your friends and family will want to have their children at the event. A phone call and frank discussion well in advance is not a bad idea.

accept it: it's expensive

I once had a bride come in for a consultation and about halfway into our conversation I learned that she was actually planning on charging guests to come to her wedding! Included in the wedding invitation was the cost to attend—$175 per person. Now, I know that most people want a nice wedding, but this was a first for me. Needless to say, I refused to plan her wedding. This is the one time in your life when it is up to you and your family to put on the event. Don't charge for tickets and don't have a cash bar.

tallying RSVPs

Create a spreadsheet that lists the names of your invited guests, their addresses, their phone numbers and e-mail addresses, the number of guests per invitation, and whether they are local or long distance. There should be a column for "yes," "no," and "maybe." Even before the invitations are mailed out, update this spreadsheet as you learn of people's plans. This will reduce your stress level greatly later on. Don't forget to include yourselves among your guest count. You would be surprised how many couples leave themselves out of the count.

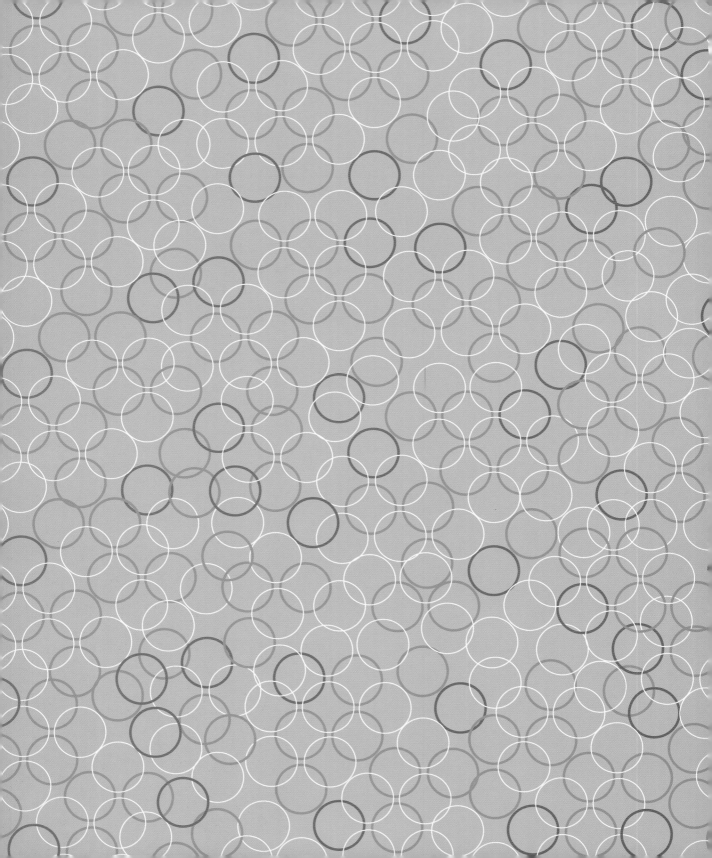

6

CHAPTER
THE GOWN

CHAPTER SIX *the gown*

Fashion designers reinvent the bridal gown every season. Those brides who require a fresh-off-the-runway look will also be looking at huge price tags. And keep in mind, by the time you head down your own catwalk the day of your wedding, your dress will already be a couple of seasons old.

To some, the search for the perfect gown is the most exciting part of the planning process; to others, it is the most overwhelming. You could begin shopping now, look until the day of your wedding, and still not see all that is available to you.

As with every facet of the wedding, I suggest looking through magazines and tearing out pages featuring gowns that appeal to you. This will give you an idea of what you like and what you don't, which translates into less wasted time for you and the sales associates at the bridal boutiques. Even if you begin shopping with a clear image of what you want, I'd still encourage you to take suggestions from the boutique's knowledgeable staff. These sales associates spend hundreds of hours researching dresses, body types, and designers. Innumerable times, a bride has rejected a style out of hand only to be stunned into purchasing it when she sees the dress on.

Today's gowns boast a variety of luxurious fabrics: silk, taffeta, damask, dupioni, organza, satin, batiste, brocade, peau de soie, rayon, tulle, and the less-often-used polyester. Consider weather and climate when selecting a fabric. Today's brides are exploring new colors and abandoning white for candlelight, champagne, maize, gold, and light shades of blue. I've even seen stunners in red. You can also count on endless degrees of formality in the current gown market.

FINDING THE RIGHT FIT

Wedding gown necklines are broken down into off the shoulder, spaghetti strap, halter, scoop, strapless, sweetheart, jewel (which has a rounded appearance), and the less-often-seen V-neck. Waist styles are basque, dropped waist, empire waist, princess cut, and natural. For bodice styles you will find corset, empire, halter, midriff, asymmetrical, princess-line, surplice, and tank.

the ball gown
traditionally features a fitted bodice with a full skirt and longer-than-average train

the empire
a high-wasted gown originally popular during the Empire period in France

the A-line
perhaps the most traditional cut, shaped in an A and cut close at the top with a fuller, elongated skirt

the ballerina
cut close on top, similar to an A-line, but has a fuller skirt with a tufted bottom cut above the shoe line

the sheath
reminiscent of old Hollywood glamour and well suited for tall, shapely women, this cut is characterized by a slim profile that fits smoothly on the body

the fish tail

perfect for the bride with narrow hips and an athletic build, this cut has a dropped waist to just above the knee and then flares out to the floor

A FEW TIPS

- An overall principle is to choose a gown that moves the silhouette as close to a proportionate hourglass figure as possible. For example, if the bride is short waisted, she should wear a drop waist. If she is petite, an empire waist will elongate her frame.
- If a bride prefers no waist in the gown, an empire or princess seam is the best choice.
- An A-line skirt is flattering for most body types.
- Many women think they cannot wear a strapless dress; however, it is truly the easiest neckline to wear. It's all in the fit. In order to keep the gown from sliding down, it should be altered to fit snuggly on the hip. It will not help to fit the gown tightly at the breast.
- When selecting couture rather than off-the-rack, expect the price tag to be *at least* $5,000. Although, don't be shocked if the cost exceeds $25,000.
- Crystals, stones, beads, pearls, jewels—embellishments are in these days. Many brides shop for a simple dress and have it custom embellished to turn an ordinary gown into a custom couture piece.
- Note that there are twelve shades of white, starting with stark white and ending in antique. When selecting your gown color, take your skin tone into account. If you are fair complected, a stark white could clash with your coloring. You are better off wearing ivories. If you have medium skin with pink tones, a creamier color may work best for you. If you have dark skin, go with white.
- Schedule a minimum of two or three fittings to get the gown perfect. Take into consideration your monthly cycle, water weight gain, and the probable temperature and humidity on your wedding day.
- Lace-up gowns will cost less since they can be tightened to provide a better fit.

MAKING THE PURCHASE

It is popular now to sample a gown and seek a designer to "knock off" your favorite, but I don't condone trying on pricey gowns you have no intention of buying. This translates to lost time and wages on the part of the boutique's staff. You should treat this industry as honestly as you want this industry to treat you. Believe me, wedding professionals share stories, and you don't want to become a red-flag bride who professionals are wary of doing business with due to underhanded behavior. Some brides, unable to select one gown, are opting for two—a more formal dress for the ceremony and a less formal one for dancing at the reception and the departure. While I find this to be a huge waste of resources and a strain on a usually tight budget, it is not my money to spend.

SHOOTING THE BRIDAL PORTRAIT

The best advice I can give is to be extremely careful if you take your gown out before the big day. Make sure that the floors are clean if the photography set is indoors. Do not walk across floors that have recently been oiled. This will permanently stain the bottom of your gown. If you are shooting outdoors, stand on a white sheet in order to eliminate staining from the elements. Grass stains do not come out of silk. Do not walk across a lawn, especially one that is wet. A rule of thumb on stains is that if it's not immediately noticeable, leave it alone. Some stains get worse with cleaning. If it is not silk, have it dry cleaned prior to the wedding. If it is silk, leave it alone. You can always use cornstarch to fade minor staining on silk, if need be.

GOWN PRESERVATION

Once your gown is selected and you are moving forward with alterations, you should decide whether you will want it to be preserved. There are companies that will take your gown after the wedding and prepare it for storage. This includes cleaning the gown (which is done with white gloves to protect the fine fabrics), pressing it, forming it onto a mold that outlines the breast and waist areas, and then boxing it up. The gown inside is rolled, instead of folded, to prevent the fabric from creasing. This makes it ready to go at a moment's notice. Most companies that do gown preservation guarantee that it will be ready to wear for up to twenty years after it is packaged. This is a wonderful way for your daughter or perhaps granddaughter to have the option of wearing this heirloom when her big day comes along in the future. You can also have the veil, gloves, and any other accessories, such as a handkerchief, done at the same time.

THE VEIL

While some brides are choosing to forgo a veil in favor of a tiara or no head dressing whatsoever, others are custom creating elaborate veils hand tooled to match their dress or décor perfectly. Veils come in a variety of lengths and styles. The fabrics traditionally used are mesh, organza, or tightly woven tulle. Some veils incorporate a blusher, a piece either attached to the veil or affixed separately that covers the face until the bride's escort raises it at the altar.

When trying on veils, style your hair the way you intend to wear it on the big day and make sure there is a way to attach the veil. It is not uncommon on the wedding day to find no method by which to secure the veil to an elaborate updo.

THE BUSTLE

There are two main types of bustles, the over-bustle and the under-bustle. The over-bustle is generally picked up on the outside and affixed by buttons, clips, or hooks on the outside of the dress. This type of bustle is typically utilized on simpler designs with a smaller and lighter train. The under-bustle, often referred to as the Victorian or French bustle, is more complicated and created by color-coded ribbons, buttons, or ties. There can be as many as twenty-four points in an elaborate bustle, but the outcome is a sophisticated look known for its scalloped effect. It is my opinion that the removable train is more trouble than it's worth. It is constantly coming unhooked or falling off. Some gowns are designed with over-bustles already sewn in and ready to go; creating an under-bustle, however, is more labor intensive. When purchasing your gown, ask the seamstress to create the bustle for you, by pinning it in place. This must be done by an experienced professional; otherwise you risk destroying the gown. Once it is complete, have the dress placed on a mannequin so you can see it clearly and photograph it for your records. The final bustle should match the photos. I advise that your planner, the maid of honor, and even your mother or mother-in-law become familiar with the bustle to ensure that more than one person knows how it should be done.

It is a good idea to have your train bustled before leaving the ceremony area. You do not want to step on it or risk getting it dirty before the reception. Make sure someone knows how the bustle is done in advance. Trust me, you don't want to rely on the groom to do this for you.

THE SHOES

The shoes should complement your gown perfectly, whether they are dyed to match the gown's fabric or bejeweled to match the gown's embellishments. The height of the heel is a personal choice, but if the groom is sensitive about his height you might want to wear a dazzling pair of flats.

There is no right or wrong shoe, as long as the bride feels comfortable and beautiful, but there are some weather-related issues that might dictate a certain style. Encapsulated-toe shoes are ideal for cooler climates or winter weddings, especially if the bride wishes to wear stockings. Open-toe pumps or sandals, preferably without stockings, are appropriate for all other seasons.

To prevent slipping, consider lightly scuffing the bottom of your shoes prior to going down the aisle. You certainly don't want to fall on your wedding day. With a scouring pad, lightly scratch the soles without removing the finish. You want to scuff them enough to create traction, but not so much that they look worn when you cross your legs. This is particularly important if you have a special embellishment on the bottom such as initials or the wedding date in stones, crystals, or paint.

I have seen so many brides with swollen feet at the end of the night. An additional pair of shoes for the reception is a life saver. Wear the fancier shoes for all of your photography, and then slip into a lower heel, an elegant pair of slippers, or bridal tennis shoes at the reception. My one request is that you do not run around in bare feet. I have seen it time and time again. There is nothing tackier than the bride or her attendants running around barefoot at a formal event. Not only is it bad form, but a barefoot bride also risks stepping on broken glass or getting her foot stepped on by a clumsy dance partner.

questions to ask when purchasing your gown

- **Do you offer complimentary alterations? What will my alteration schedule be, based on my date?** Do not let the store or company take too long and run the risk of finishing your gown too late. If there is a problem, you must be certain that there is time to correct it.
- **Can you dye shoes to match the gown?** Most companies will not have any problem with this.
- **What is your payment policy?** Be wary of companies that require full payment months before the gown is scheduled to arrive. This should also apply to couture.
- **Do you take credit cards?**
- **What is your cancellation policy?**
- **Do you deliver? If so, what is the charge?** Delivery charges can sometimes be negotiated in the purchase price.
- **What if my gown is wrong, arrives damaged, or does not fit? What are the contingency plans for this type of catastrophe?** Pay close attention to the answer here. Ask what types of issues they have had and how they corrected them. Check with the Better Business Bureau to see if there have been any complaints on this subject with this company.
- **Is there a fee for plus sizes?**
- **Are there fees associated with a rush order?**
- **How long will it take to get my gown produced and delivered after I order it?**

eating in your gown

For women who are nervous about eating in their gowns, Tidy-Bride (www.tidy-bride.com) has created a line of elegant aprons designed to look like bridal gowns. Shielding brides from unsightly drips and splatters, these wedding aprons are an ingenious idea.

questions to ask the ring salesperson or designer

• **What is your policy for cleaning the rings you sell?** You will want to have your precious rings professionally cleaned from time to time to preserve their beauty and luster. The most reputable companies will have a lifetime cleaning policy.

• **Do you charge to resize the rings, should there be a need to down the road?** This is an important question, and it is important to be realistic. Your weight could fluctuate and you'll want to make sure that your rings continue to fit.

• **What is your warranty on the rings you sell?** This goes without saying. Don't ever make a large purchase without a good warranty policy. Anything, no matter how well manufactured, can become damaged with day-to-day activities. This ring has very sentimental meaning to you, so protect it.

JEWELRY AND ACCESSORIES

The gown is the center of your ensemble. Jewelry and accessories should complement the dress, not outshine it. A simple gown might invite elaborate accessories, while a highly detailed gown might fight with bulky jewels. Often, less is best. Consider using heirloom pieces to adhere to the old and borrowed traditions. Perhaps your family has pieces that have been worn by each generation, which adds a special and personal touch. Be sure to return these heirloom pieces to the rightful owner before leaving on your honeymoon. You certainly don't want anything to happen to them.

THE RINGS

The wedding bands are selected by the bride and groom during the wedding planning process. The bride's band should complement her engagement ring and the groom's ring should complement the bride's ring. You do not necessarily have to buy a matching set, just rings that pair up nicely. If you are buying separately, chat with one another about what you both want.

On the wedding day, the bride's engagement ring should be removed before she walks down the aisle. There are different ways to handle this:

• Give the engagement ring to the groom and have him place the engagement ring on the bride's hand along with her wedding band during the ceremony.

• Give the engagement ring to the mother of the bride or maid of honor and have her return it after the ceremony.

• Wear the engagement ring on the right hand during the ceremony and then move it back to the left hand before the reception.

It is important to purchase rings made of a metal that is durable and long lasting. After all, you will hopefully wear them for the rest of your life. Gold is a precious metal, but not the most durable. Gold and silver both scratch and bend easily. You might look into platinum or the even stronger titanium, which is the strongest. Today's couples are using platinum more often than gold; however, do not be surprised by the difference in cost. A good platinum ring can be four to five times as much as a gold band.

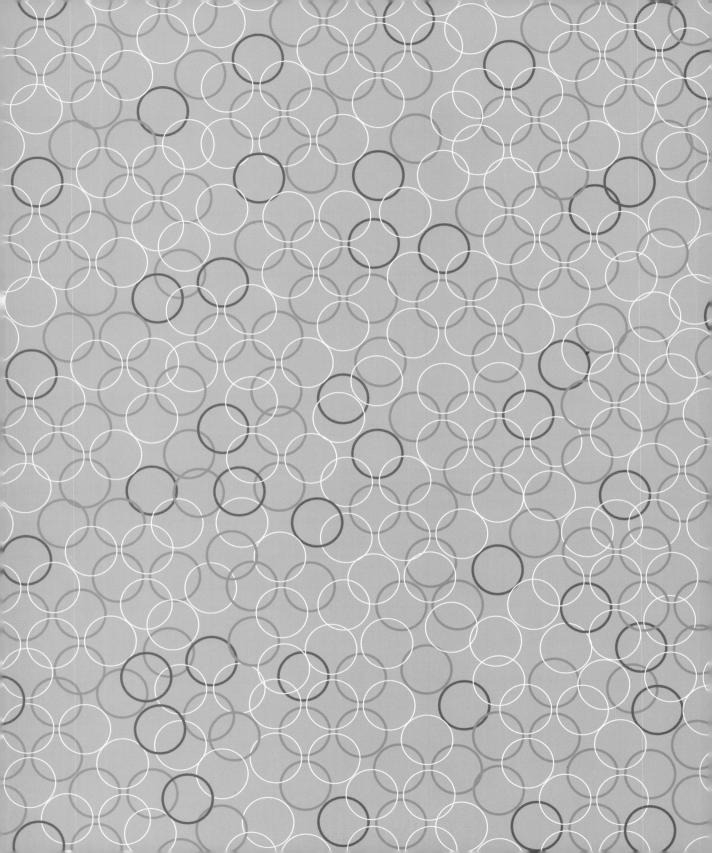

7

CHAPTER
FORMAL WEAR

CHAPTER SEVEN *formal wear*

The bride is not the only one who must be dressed perfectly on the wedding day. Her mother, her attendants, her groom, and his attendants must all look their best. If you didn't know a boutonniere should always be pinned on the left, you're not alone. Our society lives by a casual dress code, and when it's time to doll up, such questions typically arise. The following are some simple guidelines to buying, renting, and wearing party clothes.

SUITING UP

The groom's tuxedo or suit is often placed on the back burner, but because it is formal wear, adequate time must be set aside to ensure it is perfect. Some contemporary grooms opt to purchase, instead of rent, a tuxedo or suit.

When purchasing, you want to select a classic style, one that won't look outdated in a few years. I purchased tuxedos for my partner and myself prior to our holy union and was stunned when we had occasion to wear them seven times in one year. You can create many different looks by changing out shirts, pocket squares, ties, and cuff links. One good tuxedo or suit is all you really need. In the contemporary wedding climate, simple suits are becoming more popular. For a more formal look without the expense of a tuxedo, some men opt to wear suits but change out plastic buttons for black silk–covered ones.

If rental is the avenue you plan to take, there are many options. Most large formal wear–rental companies have stores in major, and some smaller, cities, which makes fitting out-of-town groomsmen much more convenient. Once a groom is fitted, the store issues him a contract number. The groomsmen will supply this contract number during their fittings to ensure their tuxedos are the proper style, cut, and price. The pre-sized tuxedo is then shipped to the destination city prior to the wedding for a final fitting and pickup. Often, larger stores offer complimentary rental to the groom if the entire wedding party rents from them as well.

BOUTONNIERES AND POCKET SQUARES

Women, children, and even the men will want a quick hug from the groom on the big day. Hug freely, but beware of crushing the fragile blossom pinned to the groom's left lapel. To avoid damaging their boutonniere, men ought to always lean in to a hug from the right.

The groom and his men will also want to keep their pocket squares from shifting about. They may want them ruffled up in a specific design or perhaps with the starched points gathered perfectly and exposed. Hang the suit jacket on a hanger and place the pocket square in the desired position. Then, fold back the coat jacket, and using a safety pin, push through and back, being careful not to expose the pin in front, and secure. Lay the lapel back down and tug on the pocket square again gently. If this is done correctly, the pocket square shouldn't budge.

GOWNS FOR MOTHERS

For the mother or stepmother of the bride or groom, this might be the most important gown purchase since her own wedding. The mothers are certainly center stage as they entertain friends and family and meet many new additions to their growing family and circle of friends.

Mothers, stepmothers, and even grandmothers have a multitude of options when seeking such a special dress. Specialty boutiques, bridal salons, major department stores, and even formal wear stores have hundreds of dresses to fit any budget or preference.

It is polite to inquire about and adhere to the color scheme set forth by the bride. If for whatever reason following the color scheme is not an option, mothers should ask the bride for an alternate color preference. It is not a bad idea for mothers to shop together or with the bride to avoid embarrassing clashes, identical purchases, or dresses the bride finds inappropriate.

For mothers who are plus size and do not feel comfortable shopping in the boutiques, advise them to head to their favorite department store or shop online. It is important to take note of exchange and refund policies in the event they do not like a dress, it is flawed, or it does not fit properly.

questions to ask the tuxedo rental store

• **How many different brands or labels of tuxedos do you offer?** Don't limit yourself. There are an incredible number of brands and options from which to choose.

• **What distinguishes one tuxedo style from another?** Take a look at the lapel and the stripe on the slacks. The width and the sheen tell a lot. Look at the cut. Is it form-fitted or blousy? Does it look tailor-made to fit or store-bought?

• **Do you have a tailor on-site who can make adjustments if the tuxedo doesn't fit perfectly when I pick it up?** Most tuxedo companies do. Do not pick up a tuxedo without trying on each component. You don't want surprises on the wedding day.

• **What are your payment and cancellation policies?** Pay close attention here.

• **Should I worry if the tuxedo colors do not match perfectly?** Yes, you should. If they cannot guarantee a perfect color match, you might consider another company.

• **Does the groom's tuxedo have to perfectly match the other tuxedos in the wedding?** Not necessarily. The basic color should match, but the style and accessories can vary.

• **Do you furnish shirts, ties, cummerbunds, vests, shoes, and accessories?** Most companies do, so you should have no problem here.

• **What is your return policy?** Most rental stores are strict about returns. They will probably want the formal wear returned before close of business the next weekday following the wedding. If you negotiate special arrangements, make sure they are in writing.

• **What if the tuxedo is damaged? What is the waiver?** Most companies have a damage waiver built into the price in case of minor imperfections when the tuxedos are returned. They will not cover major damage or destruction.

• **Is it economical to keep the tuxedo for use on my honeymoon if it is required?** You might find that in this case purchasing a tuxedo is a more reasonable option.

OUTFITTING BRIDESMAIDS

The "bridesmaid's dress" used to be a scary thing, but in recent years, designers have created fabulous options. There are thousands you would want to wear again.

Dress length is a critical consideration when selecting your attendants' gowns. If the wedding is formal, a full-length dress is required. In an afternoon, casual, or beach wedding, tea length is more appropriate.

If your bridal party has a variety of body types, I suggest finding a skilled tailor or seamstress to custom design and construct your attendants' clothing. This way, you can select the color, fabric, and even styles for them to choose from. Options might create a happier wedding party, as no two bodies look the same in a dress. Some designer bridal lines have caught on to this concept and are offering an extensive array of separates in the same color.

Your color scheme will play a large part in the selection of the bridesmaids' attire. If you are looking for a solid color, make sure all the dresses are cut from the same dye lot. There can be tremendous variances, and side by side, this will be noticeable. If you have bridesmaids who live out of town, have them send you a fabric swatch to make certain the dresses match perfectly.

If you do not find what you are looking for in bridal salons and boutiques, another option is the formal wear section of your favorite department store. You will not find the variety in the same color, but some brides are opting for black full-length dresses of the bridesmaids' choosing. This is another easy way for out-of-town attendants to buy their dresses: a style number and phone call to the department store in their area will ensure the correct dress is ordered.

After taking such pains to find the perfect dresses, don't drop the ball on shoes and accessories. Some brides insist on each person wearing the same exact shoe, a pair dyed to match, or a shoe that complements the gown. Others allow each attendant to select her own shoe. Depending on your need for a unified look, shoes may or may not be an issue. Inexpensive jewelry is a lovely gift item and the perfect way to create a cohesive look for the bridal party. Most boutiques, bridal and otherwise, offer a large range of costume options for formal and informal occasions.

THE FLOWER GIRL'S DRESS

Originally, the job of the flower girl was to spread grain at the feet of the bride to promote fertility and happiness in the marriage. Today, little ones toss rose petals to create a lovely path for the bride as she begins her new life. This has become more of an honorary position and a perfect way to include young children in the ceremony.

As with other formal wear, you will be stunned by the number of options for this special dress. It is nice to find a dress that not only fits into the wedding scheme but also can be worn several times before it's outgrown. It is never a bad idea to take the flower girl with you on this most momentous outing. Although it may be hectic to shop with a little girl, ultimately her happiness with her dress can translate into her happiness the day of the wedding. Keep ease of dressing in mind when making your selection, as well as ease of undressing. I've seen a couple of flower girls cast off their trappings in favor of only tights and shoes! Allowing the child to wear the special dress a few times before the wedding—perhaps to a tea party, with no tea of course—could help her feel more comfortable.

THE RING BEARER'S ATTIRE

The ring bearer's attire can be rented at the same store where the groom and groomsmen are suited. Do not be afraid to have some fun with the ring bearer's suit. If all the men are wearing standard tuxedos, you can purchase or rent a tux for the ring bearer with tails or even a morning suit jacket. These little guys are adorable when they are dressed up wearing grown up attire, and the guests love it.

8

CHAPTER

THE WEDDING PARTY

CHAPTER EIGHT *the wedding party*

Selecting the bridal party is often an exercise in appeasing others. When feelings of anxiety begin to creep up, try to focus on the fact that you are marrying your best friend and that everyone else is simply there as a support system.

Now is the era of unconventional wedding parties. Don't be afraid to fly in the face of tradition. I have seen ex-husbands and gay men stand up as the "maid of honor," as well as five best men and no actual groomsmen.

It is my theory that the size of the wedding party should be proportionate to the size of the event. If you are having fifty people for an intimate ceremony, it would feel overwhelming to have every member of your sorority stand up with you. On the flip side, a large guest list would perfectly balance a large wedding party. Either way, there are no hard-and-fast rules.

Do not feel pressured to have balance; again, your wedding party choices should be personal and a reflection of those closest to you.

As you select people who are significant in your life, try to avoid selecting anyone who will cause you anxiety. Part of the role of the bridal party is to keep the bride and groom calm and relaxed before the ceremony. If you include a high-maintenance friend, he or she will be a high-maintenance member of the bridal party. Make your choices carefully, and count on hurt feelings. They are going to happen.

HOUSE PARTY AND USHERS

The house party has two purposes: to help with small details and to include meaningful people in an honorary role. House party tasks can be anything—attending the guest book, cleaning the bride's room after the ceremony, managing the veil before and after the ceremony, handing out programs. I have found, in most cases, that the house party feels less significant than the bridal party; instead of feeling honored, they feel slighted and put upon. Bridesmaids can manage and assist with your attire and the cleanup, and programs can be left on each seat or placed on the sign-in table—people know to look for them.

Ushers are the male counterpart to the house party. Having ushers is optional. Certainly, guests can seat themselves, but it is a lovely tradition for the women to be escorted to their seats. When selecting men for usher duty, pick outgoing, friendly, and responsible friends or relatives, as they will likely be guests' first impression of the event. The number of ushers should correspond directly with the number of guests. I suggest no less than one usher per fifty guests, as they can easily seat this number in thirty minutes, which is the typical pre-ceremony seating time allotment. If you are short on ushers to meet this requirement, you can pull one or two of the groomsmen to fill in. Just don't pull all the men away from the groom. They are as important to him as the bridesmaids are to the bride during the moments leading up to the processional.

THE OFFICIANT

The minister, priest, rabbi, or other officiant will generally require a pre-wedding consultation. If he or she does not, you should insist on one. It is this person who will share center stage with you at the ceremony, and you want to be certain that you like his or her demeanor, personality, and officiating style. Additionally, you will want to make sure that the selected officiant suits your ceremony. Although some have nonnegotiable elements, most will offer you some room for personalization. This is your ceremony and should, to some degree, reflect you as a couple, your family, and your faith.

As an expression of their relationship, some couples choose to write their own vows. I find this to be a lovely personal touch and have a few suggestions to help avoid anxiety. First, begin the writing process well in advance of the wedding to give adequate time for your heart and mind to come up with the perfect words to exchange. If you are having difficulty, check the Internet or visit the library for inspiration. Countless books and Web sites are devoted to wedding vows and toasts. There is no need to plagiarize; often all you need is a prompt or some inspiration to verbalize your feelings.

Although you may have an excellent memory, the nervous energy of standing in front of all of your family and friends may cause you to forget the words you planned to say. If you are uncertain about your ability to memorize your vows, I recommend that you write them down on a small card and slip it into your gown, inner pocket, or entrust the card to the best man, maid of honor, or officiant. The impact will not be diminished if you read your vows or repeat them after the officiant.

questions to ask a potential wedding officiant

- **Do you conduct interfaith marriages?** Of course, ask this if it pertains to your situation.
- **Will you marry us if one or both of us have been divorced?** Most will these days. If you've been divorced and the officiant answers "no" to this question, simply move on to someone else.
- **Will you marry us if we are not members of the congregation? If not, what are the requirements to become a member? Is there a waiting period before you will marry us after we join the congregation?**
- **Do you require premarital or religious counseling? If so, what does that entail?**
- **Would you allow another officiant (of another religion or a family member) to assist with the ceremony?**
- **What is your fee and payment policy?**
- **What is your cancellation policy?**
- **Do you attend and orchestrate the rehearsal? If so, is there an extra fee for this service?**
- **Do you normally receive a gratuity in addition to your fee?**
- **How long will the ceremony last?**

GIFTS

Wedding gifts include gifts placed in hotel rooms to greet your friends and family, as well as the attendant gifts, the gifts to thank your family for hosting your wedding, and the all-important bride and groom gift exchange.

Attendant gifts, family gifts, and the gifts that the bride and groom give one another are typically exchanged at the rehearsal dinner. If you have purchased necklaces that you want your bridesmaids to wear on the big day, this is the perfect time to pass them out. For the groomsmen, a power pen, a pair of cuff links, a money clip, or even a good cigar makes a great gift.

For hotel guests, rather than give them something that needs to be packed up and hauled home, consider giving them a gift bag of bottled spring water and snacks. You might also include fragrant candles, bath accessories, or flowers to make their room smell fresh and feel less like a hotel. Guests may also appreciate a personalized note from the bride and groom, maps, directions to the ceremony and reception, and a wedding-weekend itinerary. Since I live in Dallas, we often use Texas-themed gifts, such as a wicker cowboy hat. Don't be afraid to get creative and invite your attendants to help you. Note that some hotels will charge a fee to deliver these to your guests' rooms. Regardless, tip the concierge for taking care of this and make every attempt to have this done before the guests' arrival.

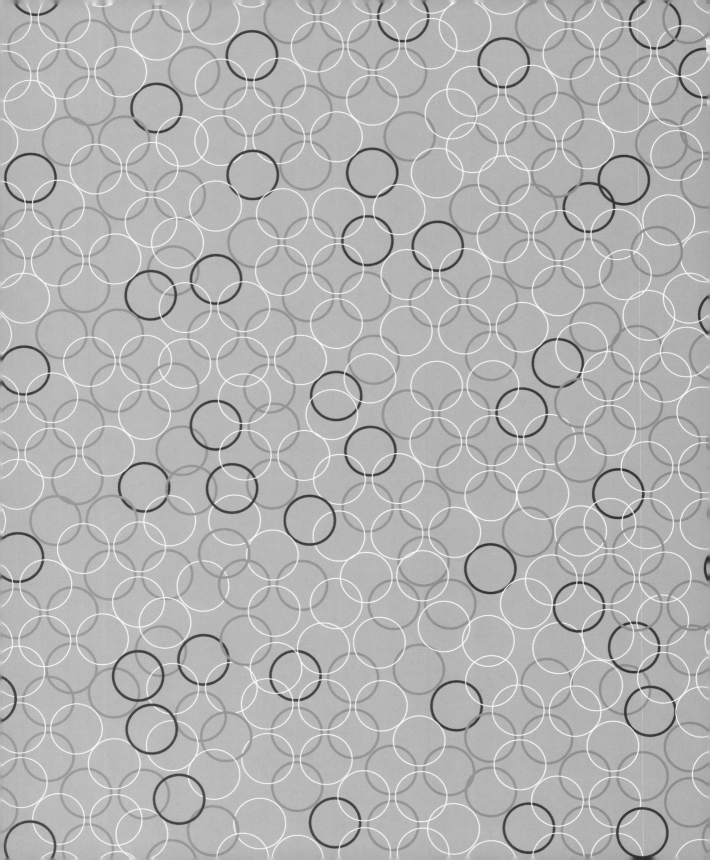

9

CHAPTER
FOOD AND DRINK

CHAPTER NINE *food and drink*

Perhaps the most important aspect of your reception beyond the venue and décor is the food and beverages you serve your guests. The options can range from a spread of pastries to lavish feasts, depending on the length of your event, the time of day, the season, and, most significantly, the budget.

When determining the menu, consider the length of the event and whether guests will expect a full meal. If the event occurs during traditional meal hours, 8–10 AM for breakfast, 11 AM–1 PM for lunch, or 5–9 PM for dinner, you need to serve the equivalent of a meal. When estimating the length of your event, take into consideration the travel time to the ceremony, the length of the ceremony, and then the entire reception.

If you are having a morning ceremony and reception between the hours of a meal, light appetizers or buffet-style brunch items and cake will suffice. A ceremony and reception that occurs between the lunch and dinner hour can be handled with a buffet or passed hors d'oeuvres. I always recommend having a variety of cheeses, fruits, and vegetables in addition to light hors d'oeuvres and cake. Any event after 5 PM will likely last, at minimum, through the dinner hour, so you are expected to feed your guests the equivalent of a meal. Many venues offer what are considered "heavy appetizers": jumbo prawns, giant stuffed mushrooms, beef medallions, mini soup servings in shot glasses, and crudités. The options are endless and ideal for a short event, but you should offer guests a full meal if it will be too late for them to dine on their own after the reception. If you do not provide your guests with enough food, they will leave early in search of more. This could undermine all your efforts to host a lovely party celebrating your marriage. If you need to reallocate money from another area of the budget to make certain you offer a suitable amount of food, this must be done.

THE FOOD

There are a number of ways to structure a reception, but many begin with a cocktail hour during which hot and cold appetizers are available or passed. This is a lovely way to whet the guests' appetites and keep them from becoming tipsy before the reception. Four to five appetizers per person is a safe average.

Dinner can be offered as a buffet or at stations, which give guests a number of food choices. A buffet ensures that people will be up and mingling from the start. Keep in mind, if you select a buffet-style dinner, venues may not automatically give you capacity seating (see page 22). Furthermore, the tables may not be set, which means when your guests walk in, they will enter to tables with only centerpieces and linens. If you would prefer everyone to have an actual seat and place setting, you will likely confront a per-person charge.

A seated dinner is certainly a more formal option. The tables are set, each person has a seat, no one has to stand in line, and it is easy to intersperse toasting or show a short video, if you wish.

Regardless of the type of dinner you choose, the food you select should offer a good variety of meat, vegetables, and starch. Adding a few extra vegetarian options will please everyone. If you are serving cake, no additional dessert needs to be added to the menu, unless you are interested in a chocolate fountain or some other complementary wedding fare, such as a dessert or Venetian station, an intermezzo, or action stations for Bananas Foster or Cherries Jubilee.

VENDOR MEALS

In some cases, the planner and assistants, as well as the band or DJ, the photographer and videographer, and their respective staffs, will have been with you since the beginning of the day. Please don't starve the people who are working tirelessly behind the scenes to perfect your special event.

Plan to feed these important staff members and any other vendors who remain on hand throughout the dinner hour, with the exception of the catering staff, who will be fed before your dinner. You do not need to seat vendors in the dining room or offer them the same fare you are enjoying. Since many vendors find it awkward to take part in the buffet line, you might ask your venue if they have additional space for a small dining area. A mini-buffet, deli tray, duplicate meals, or box meals for your professionals will go a long way in saying thank you.

THE KIDDIES' TABLE

Unless you specified an adult-only reception, you will undoubtedly have children in attendance. It is polite and worthwhile to cater to them a bit. Children's tables can be set with lollipop and candy centerpieces, coloring books, and crayons. I have also seen a few Nintendo Game Boys or other pocket games added to the mix. The happier they are and the busier they are, the lower the chance their parents will feel pressed to leave early.

Many children are picky eaters, so you might ask your caterer to prepare a second buffet or plate for children consisting of classic favorites, such as macaroni and cheese, pizza, chicken fingers, French fries, fruit, cheese, chips, vegetables, and pasta. This will alleviate any frustration on the part of the parents trying to feed their child.

It is becoming increasingly popular and economical to request a room close to your venue for children's entertainment. Some hotels offer a nanny service, or you can hire sitters who come from an agency or who are highly recommended by friends. Video games, movies, toys, music, reading, dancing, and snacks are all welcome distractions from the boring adult event. Be sure to let your guests with children know ahead of time that there will be supervised children's activities and a play area. Having these options may decrease the number of declines on your guest list.

questions to ask the catering manager

• **Do you offer a complimentary tasting?** Reputable companies do. Don't expect a tasting prior to booking, however. It is not prudent for venues to offer a free lunch to everyone who inquires about an event. But once you have booked your event, schedule a tasting and send a list of the things you would like to try off their catering menu. Usually you select about six to eight hors d'oeuvres, two to three salads, two soups, and three entrees for a seated dinner. For a buffet, you will sample two to three options per category.

• **What guarantee do I have that the food at the reception will be as good as the food I select at my tasting?**
This is where referrals from those who have had food from this venue before will come in handy.

• **What is your payment plan and cancellation policy?**

• **Is your food prepared on-site or elsewhere and then transported?**
Although the food may be properly prepared in an off-site kitchen, a good medium-rare steak quickly becomes medium-well in a warming cabinet.

• **Do you have a gratuity and service charge? If so, what is the percentage?** Every venue has a different charge. Make sure you include it in your budget when weighing the options of the caterer. Tax must be added too. If there is a 22 percent service charge and an 8 percent tax, you have to add 30 percent on top of every published price in their menu proposal.

BEVERAGES

Each facility will likely have a food and beverage minimum. If after selecting medium- to low-priced menu items you are still having trouble staying within your budget, you might take a look at the beverages you are serving.

If you find you need to eliminate alcohol to feed everyone, know upfront that guests will leave early. One cost-cutting option is to offer only beer and wine, but a facility can often pour hard liquor much cheaper than beer and wine, depending on the brand or type of alcohol used. Make certain the difference in price is worth it. You might offer one signature drink in addition to beer and wine. This drink could be the couple's favorite, or perhaps the color of the cocktail blends well with the décor.

The "call" or "house" bar is another less expensive bar alternative. With this option you determine the quality of alcohol served. You can always keep a bottle of the good stuff behind the bar for yourselves. The next step up is "premium" or "top shelf" and features more expensive brands of alcohol, and finally "prestige" offers other options such as brandy, cognac, and more complicated mixed drinks.

Martini bars or specialty drink bars are gaining popularity. I once planned an event that had cocktail tables set up with different bottles of liquors, and shot glasses were passed around with lemons and limes. On one table we had vodka and Frangelico; on another we served vodka and Kahlua; several other tables poured different tequilas. Venue rules and space limitations will dictate the feasibility of this concept.

Be careful not to underestimate the number of cocktails your friends and family will order. Your wedding is a celebration and many guests who rarely drink will partake on your special day. Payment options vary among venues, but most offer the choice of either a "consumption" bar or a "package" bar. With a consumption bar, you pay for the actual number of drinks consumed. This seems like a good idea, but I have seen couples hit with hefty bills after the event. If you choose a consumption bar, you ought to pre-authorize the catering manager to continue serving past the drink estimate. You don't want to be faced with shutting down the bar hours before the event is scheduled to end because your guests have consumed the prepaid number of beverages. Personally I recommend selecting a "package" bar, which charges per person rather than per drink. The venue will charge one up-front fee, and if your guests drink more than the venue's estimate you won't receive an additional bill. In both cases, a payment option must be determined before the event and the venue will offer you an estimate that you can factor into your food and beverage minimum.

If you are planning to have wine poured at dinner, ask if there is an additional fee or if the wine served tableside is included in your package. This is a nice option and it keeps your guests from having to leave their dinner to go to the bar for a drink.

There are a number of ways to handle the champagne toasts, but you need to determine whether champagne is included in your package. Champagne can be passed before the toast, which I do not recommend since many people won't drink it, or guests can toast you with whatever beverage they happen to be consuming at the time.

Once again, whatever decisions you make regarding alcohol, please don't offer a cash bar. It is tacky and rude to invite guests to your wedding and not offer them a free drink. If consumption of alcohol is against your religion or you don't have the budget for an open bar, eliminate alcohol entirely. Either way, nonalcoholic beverages should always be on hand for the children and nondrinkers.

• **Do you offer a complimentary tasting?**
Reputable companies do. Do not purchase a cake
from a bakery that does not taste good or is not
structurally sound. If they cannot control these
issues in their bakery during an appointment,
it is unlikely they will be able to on the wedding
day at another location.

• **How far in advance of the wedding do you
bake and ice the cake?** This answer can have
a great deal to do with the freshness and
moistness of the cake at your wedding. Do
not contract with a company that gives you
an answer that is more than three days prior
to the wedding.

• **Do you deliver and what is the charge?**

• **How will you guarantee the cake at my event
will be as good as the cake I have at my tasting?** This is where referrals will come in handy
from those who have had cake at an event from
this bakery.

• **What is your payment plan and cancellation
policy?**

• **Will you create a custom design cake or
does it have to be from your portfolio?** It is
your wedding. You should not be required to
purchase a cake design that has been used for
another wedding. After all, you want your
wedding to be unique.

• **Do you charge for pillars, cake plateaus, and
toppers?**

• **Do you have to use fondant on cakes in the
warmer months?** This answer should be no. You
do not have to have a cake with fondant if you do
not want it.

• **Is your cake baked from scratch or a mix?**
Hopefully you will get an accurate answer here.
You can usually tell the difference at the tasting.

• **Are your frostings and fillings pre-made or
homemade?** Pre-made frostings are usually
constructed with a large amount of shortening
and can be a nightmare in warm weather. You
certainly don't want your cake to capsize during
your reception!

THE WEDDING CAKE

Nothing says "Welcome to my reception!"
like a majestic, multi-tiered wedding cake.
I like to place it near the entrance so it can
be admired immediately. Another option is to
station the cake under the chuppah or canopy
where the couple stood as they exchanged
vows at the ceremony.

The first step, however, is to taste some cake. You will
undoubtedly be stunned by the options during your first tasting.
Wedding cakes are not just white cake anymore. Expect
flavors such as white chocolate, Italian crème, pink champagne, red velvet, hazelnut, German chocolate, carrot, and so
many more I cannot possibly list them. These flavors may be
enhanced with fruit fillings, mousses, and liqueurs. Amaretto
and Grand Marnier are two popular liqueurs that add flavor
as well as maintain moisture. Frostings are the finishing
touch, and the options go beyond butter cream. One modern
frosting is called fondant, which can be formed into elaborate
shapes, making the cake look like a work of art. Your cakes
should be appealing to you as well as your guests, who will
have been ogling it for hours.

In the South, there is a long-standing tradition of serving a
groom's cake. This can be a surprise from the bride or selected
by the groom himself. These cakes tend to reflect the groom's
personality, favorite dessert, hobby, or passion. The options
are endless. I've ordered cakes in the shape and flavor of a
Reese's Peanut Butter Cup, an enormous cupcake, an Almond
Joy, and a Hostess Sno Ball. I've helped couples design cakes
shaped like a Black Hawk helicopter, a poodle, a Dallas Cowboys star, the entire University of Texas stadium, and a record
with an edible image of Bono and U2. The stunner of my
career was a twelve-foot cake with a sugar sculpture of the
bride, in her gown, popping out of the top.

No one says you have to go crazy with either cake, and
many brides object to the groom's cake because it often
clashes with the carefully crafted décor of the reception. My
answer to this is to give the groom his own cake ceremony following the cutting of the bride's cake. Ask the staff to wheel in
the groom's cake and make a huge production for him. It is a
nice way to shine the light on the groom and give him his own
special moment. If the cake pays homage to his alma mater,
consider playing the school's fight song.

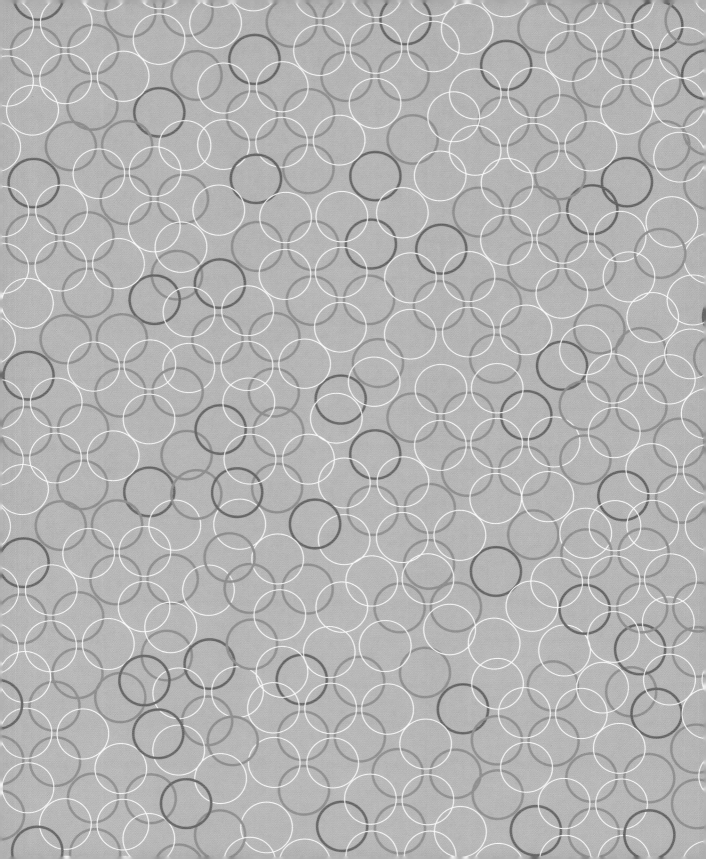

10
CHAPTER
DECOR

CHAPTER TEN *décor*

Many brides place flowers and décor at the top of their priority list. The décor is what separates one wedding from another. From lighting and linens to decorative rentals and centerpieces, each element brings you one step closer to creating a magical ambiance and making a lasting impression on your guests.

SHOPPING FOR FLOWERS

With the variety in today's floral market, you may find decision making to be daunting. Your florist will help you with wedding colors if you have not already done this on your own or with your wedding planner. Once a color scheme is selected, the floral designer will show you what is available. A good florist can tell you which flowers will be in season at the time of your event, how stem pricing will vary seasonally, and whether the blooms are grown domestically or shipped from another country.

Typically, the bride gives flowers to the mothers, fathers, grandmothers, grandfathers, as well as siblings who are not in the wedding party and other close family members. Mothers have traditionally worn a corsage, but this has gone out of style because women don't want to mar their expensive designer gowns and suits. Pin-on corsages are heavy and can easily damage fine fabrics, so a small bouquet or nosegay is more widely accepted. Grandmothers still cling to tradition, and in many cases wear the pin-on variety. House party members usually wear a wrist corsage or an embellished boutonniere.

THE CEREMONY FLORAL

Most couples embellish their ceremonies with flowers—altar and pew floral arrangements, bouquets, boutonnieres, nosegays, corsages, garlands, wreaths. If your ceremony is in a church, the church coordinator will most likely have a list of the sanctuary's rules and regulations. If you are holding the ceremony in a nonreligious location, the sky's the limit.

One question brides ask me frequently is how much flowers for a wedding ceremony typically cost? There are industry standards, but with so many types of floral design businesses and options available, the prices vary widely. However, to help you budget, here are some price estimates:

• **The bride's bouquet** can be designed in a number of ways. There are round, cascading or teardrop, and even arm bouquets like the ones beauty pageant winners hold while walking down the runway. The flowers can also be designed in bouquet holders (which are incredibly out of style), wired-stem arrangements, or the more common and current hand-tied method. With all of this in mind, prices can range from $50 to $500, with most brides paying somewhere around $175.

• **The bridesmaids' bouquets** are generally simpler than the bride's and fall within the price range of $35–$90, with an average of $75.

• **Boutonnieres** can cost between $7 and $20, but most run around $12.

• **Corsages** average around $35.

• **Altar designs** can set you back about $200–$500 each. There are countless container choices and creative ways to coordinate these larger arrangements with the wedding party's bouquets. You can have two or more altar designs, depending on the facility and its guidelines. You generally want to place floral arrangements symmetrically on the altar to frame the wedding party during the ceremony.

• **A chuppah** is basically a gazebo or four columns with a fabric top. The Jewish faith considers this a representation of the stable house the couple will live in during their marriage. The fabric is often handed down from generation to generation. Flowers can be used to embellish the top, the sides, or the base. Chuppahs vary in price from $600 to $7,000, depending on the complexity of the design and the amount of floral added for decorative purposes.

matching the bouquet to the gown

Once your wedding dress has been cut down during alteration, take the excess fabric to your floral designer and have him or her use it to finish the bouquet handle. This is a great way to tie the bouquet beautifully to your gown.

a floral keepsake

If you are sentimental, consider preserving your bridal bouquet after the event. Generally there are several bridal bouquets: one for walking down the aisle, one for photographs, and one to toss at the reception. Choose your favorite, or the least damaged, and request that your floral designer freeze-dry it.

It's an interesting process. The bouquet is photographed from every angle, and then taken apart. The blooms are cut off, mounted on a wire, affixed to a tray, and then placed in a chamber where they are slowly frozen and dried for several months. When they come out, they look like fragile representations of the fresh blooms. These are not like flowers dried upside down. They hold their natural shape and usually their color. The bouquet is then re-created to look as it did on the day of your wedding and placed in a vessel, such as a tabletop dome or the more traditional shadow box. It's an expensive process, but the bouquet will last a lifetime.

questions to ask your
floral designer and decorator

• **How do you guarantee that I will receive the floral types and quality that were determined in my consultation?**

• **Does your contract outline the individual floral stems that I want used in my designs?** If not, you are likely not going to get what you think you're ordering. It is imperative that the contract include extensive details about each floral piece. Ask about their replacement policy if there is a problem actually getting the stems that you ordered.

• **How many weddings do you take on in a weekend?** This is an important question. Many floral design companies take on more weddings than they can actually accommodate, which overburdens their facility, cooler space, staffing, delivery personnel, and delivery vehicle capacity. Only book those vendors who can honestly promise that you'll receive the attention you deserve on your wedding day.

• **Do you accept payment and installment plans? What is the deposit to hold my date?**

• **After my consultation, how long will you hold a date for me without a deposit?** If you don't book on the spot, never assume that a designer will hold your date.

• **What is your cancellation policy? What is your date-change policy?**

• **How much creative freedom does your company give its designers?** You may be working with a talented designer but if the company heavily restricts what supplies its designers can order, you may not get the décor that you want. Assess whether the company has antiquated ideas about to how to produce a wedding and whether its business practices will impede your high standards.

• **Do you personally attend the set-up at the wedding ceremony and reception?** Many designers regularly meet with you during the planning process but then send delivery drivers to set up the event. Insist that the designer attend your event to ensure the set-up goes smoothly.

THE RECEPTION FLORAL

When you meet with a floral designer, bring your wedding notebook with you. Flip through the magazine clippings that you've collected and browse through any available photographs of the florist's past work. As you share your ideas, pay close attention to the floral designer's reactions. You need a floral designer who is onboard with your vision, someone who understands what you want and knows how to get the job done. Designers who seem uncomfortable or unenthusiastic probably aren't right for your event.

Money is also a factor. When selecting a floral and décor vendor you should choose the person and company who can create your look for a reasonable price (based on the items that you are ordering). Finding the best deal usually requires meeting with several florists for consultations before deciding on one.

Floral options for your reception can consist of centerpieces, candles, entry décor, guest-book-table flowers (where we usually put the toss bouquet), floral chandeliers, buffet arrangements, transferred altar designs, and anything else your heart desires.

THE RECEPTION DECOR

The days of the "mom-and-pop" floral store have come to an end. When grocery stores and large shopping chains began selling a variety of flowers at deep discounts, the traditional cash-and-carry floral business couldn't compete. To survive, many floral designers have diversified to offer complete turn-key event décor services.

This surge of diversity offered by traditional wedding florists has been a great boon for the modern bride. Professional florists have the edge when it comes to employing creative and well-trained designers; discount stores hire designers, but not of the same caliber. At today's florist, you can rent linens, lighting, and decorative rentals that will elevate your wedding to the level of any celebrity event.

linens

Linens are a good place to begin when developing your reception's decorative scheme. Fabrics can establish a palette that will inspire the rest of the décor. Today's bride no longer has to settle for the venue's shoddy polyester linens. Rental companies offer an array of tablecloths, chair covers, napkins, overlays, chair caps and ties, and much more. These linen choices come in a plethora of silks, satins, brocades, taffetas, sheers, and organza fabrics. The different color and pattern options are so wide you should have no problem finding sets to fit your taste.

Some linen companies will even create custom designs for you and then add your design to their portfolio as a rental option for future clients. If you want custom linen, start by either designing it yourself or by asking an artist to design a pattern for you. Once you've drawn your vision, submit it to the linen company. Just know that ultimately they are the ones who will decide whether your design suits their line and merits production.

draperies

Imagine scrimming a ballroom in white silk with rear lighting that casts a saffron glow over your wedding reception. Draperies are an economical way to cover your venue's unsightly walls or permanent décor. You can even create a tent-like effect indoors with pipe and draped fabric. Just make sure your drapery company follows these three important guidelines:

• Use fabric with an appropriate translucency. If you want total coverage and no visual bleed, don't use organza or sheers, although rear lighting is easier to cast through these fabrics. Also remember that color can be severe. We often use white or ivory fabric and let the light do the coloring.

• Make sure the pipe and drape company uses covers to hide those hideous steel poles. Not disguising the poles is unacceptable and can easily ruin an expensive décor scheme.

• Let the fabric puddle at the floor and hang the draperies as high as possible, based on the limitations of the room.

lighting

So many people overlook lighting. Yes, your facility probably has installed lighting: There are likely chandeliers, wall sconces, or strategically placed recessed lighting fixtures. However, for one night this venue becomes your space, and it should be lit in a way that enhances the personality of your event. Lighting is a way to amplify the parts of the room you like and eliminate those components you do not. Dim the house lights to create ambiance and use lighting effects to highlight parts of the room you want your guests to notice.

Lighting can flood an array of colors into a room. When selecting "wash" lighting, consider how the color will alter the look of the flowers, the linens, and, most importantly, your skin tone and gown. Will a purple wash work with your wine-colored silk tablecloths? Probably not. Purple lighting will likely make the linens look black. Plus, do you really want everyone at your reception to look purple? Personally, I prefer skin tone washes such as pinks, peaches, ivories, and soft whites. There is a wash called "flesh tone," which is a blend of peaches and pinks that gives everyone's complexion a warm, healthy glow. After all, you must look your absolute best at your wedding, and the lighting has a huge impact. You can vary the effect of wash lighting during the course of the evening by using intelligent lighting that changes colors slowly during the reception.

Another lighting component is "pin" lighting, which are lights that can be focused on the dining table or on beautiful centerpieces. This way, the room can be lit dramatically, but guests will still be able to see the food on their plates.

There is also "gobo" lighting, which is a metal plate that fits on the light fixture to cast an image. I use this a lot to project the bride and groom's names, initials, or custom-designed wedding logo onto the wall or dance floor. The custom-designed gobo is yours to keep after the event and could be used for a future anniversary party or renewal of vows in years to come.

decorative rentals

Perhaps you want an antique chandelier hung over the dance floor or dozens of paper lanterns hung from the ceiling. Or maybe you envision an elaborate cake table design at the reception or a bamboo tiki bar at the rehearsal dinner. Every designer will have creative ideas for using decorative rentals at your event.

Keep in mind that guests will appreciate a comfortable place to sit and relax at the reception. I often rent furniture for seating arrangements around the dance floor and cocktail area, or to create a luxurious lounge in a connecting room. I've also constructed gazebos and archways with benches. When it comes to decorative rentals, the possibilities are truly endless.

PARTY FAVORS

In the past, guests took pieces of wedding cake home and put them under their pillows for good luck—a tradition I've never understood. However, it is a wonderful gesture to send your guests home with a treat—perhaps a small box of truffles, a chocolate menu card, or fortune cookies with a message from the bride and groom on the slip of paper. Recently, I had a bride who gave lottery scratch-off tickets, which was a fun gift. The best favors hook into the theme of the wedding: perhaps fire-roasted pecans from the bride's home state or a wine bottle stopper for a reception at a vineyard. If you have a fountain in the reception venue, give each guest a shiny new coin to toss into the fountain for good luck. Or wrap sets of two Bosc pears in decorative mesh and attach a tag inscribed with the bride and groom's names and the words "a perfect pair." Whatever your selection, take the time to think of something creative. If your wedding favors are an afterthought, they will look like one.

The packaging of the favor is as important as the gift itself. It should coordinate with the reception décor and be personalized in some way. The bride and groom's initials, an engagement photo, or a custom logo is a nice touch. For instance, if the favor is a mini-bottle of champagne, create a custom bottle label or attach a monogrammed gift tag to each.

If you don't put the favors beside each place setting at dinner, consider placing them on the guest book table. We often set up a candy station on this table during the reception so that guests can take home small bags of their favorite sweets.

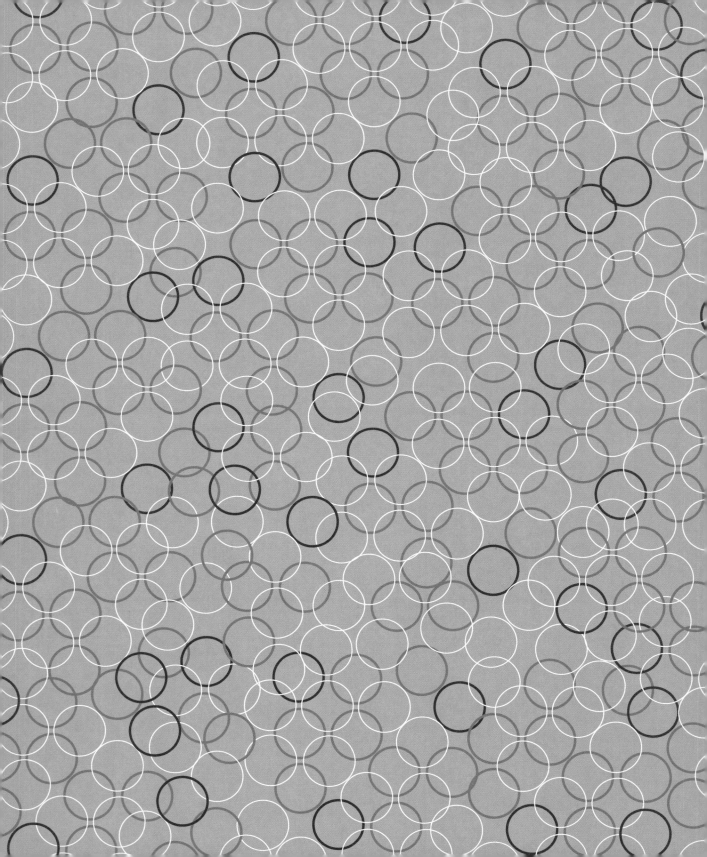

CHAPTER

PHOTOGRAPHY
AND VIDEOGRAPHY

11

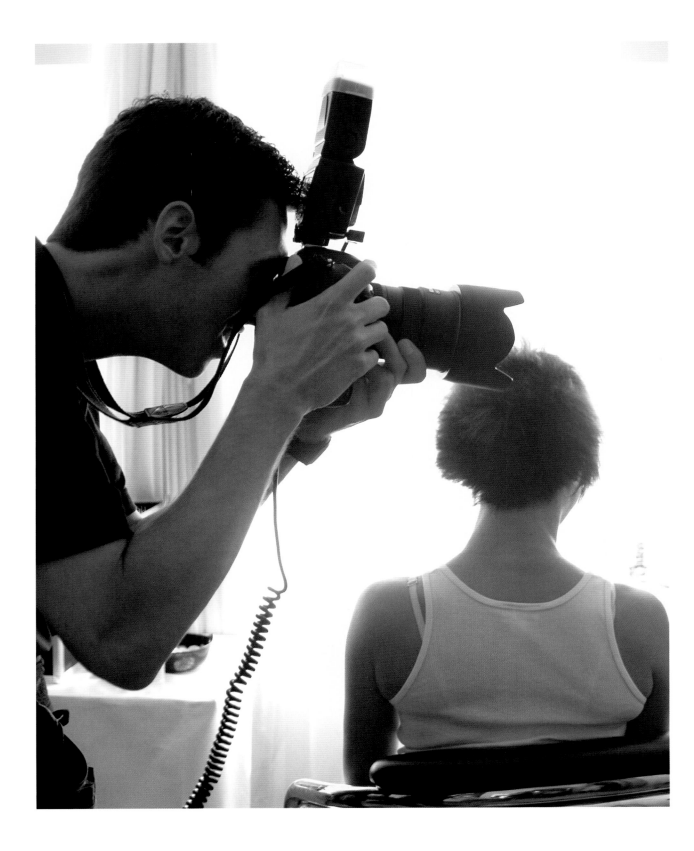

CHAPTER ELEVEN *photography and videography*

I once read an article that listed the top ten over-paid professionals. Number one was wedding photographer. Annoyed, I e-mailed the writer and asked him to name the best day of his life. His response: his wedding day. He saw his error immediately.

On the most important day of *your* life, it is imperative to hire a professional. Your wedding photographer should be someone who shoots full-time, not someone who dabbles with the craft on weekends. A professional should have at least two cameras and a variety of lenses and flashes. Make sure you see all of it before the wedding. Also, don't undervalue the importance of a degree in fine art photography. Hiring an amateur to shoot your big day is tantamount to hiring a beauty school dropout to cut and color your hair the morning of your wedding. Your wedding day is not a day to gamble.

A good photographer will have a combination of credentials earned in the classroom and experience gained in the field. There are commercial photographers, photojournalists, and fashion photographers, among others. On your wedding day, you want a wedding photographer, one who works mostly in the wedding field, and the more experience he or she has, the better. Two years versus ten is significant. With each new challenge comes more experience, and an experienced photographer will confidently handle the unpredictable nature of a wedding. Each event is entirely different, with unforeseeable challenges—family dynamics, weather, location, lighting, the temperament of the bride, the timing of the reception setup. Hiring a professional is critical.

WHAT SHOULD I EXPECT OF MY PHOTOGRAPHER?

The duties of a professional wedding photographer are myriad. Since he or she will spend most of the day in close contact with the bride, personality is a major factor. Sit down and visit with your potential photographer. Make sure you like her personality and appreciate her sense of humor. A photographer who is overbearing, demanding, pushy, or inappropriate can taint a wedding. Discuss the type of images you envision. View albums of the photographer's past work. Typically, photographers take hundreds of images of one event. Do not settle for ten to fifteen shots from each wedding; ask to view a couple hundred. This will give you a strong overview of the style and the technical savvy of the photographer. If he will only share with you a small sampling, it's fair to assume that a good number of images from the event did not turn out well.

Photographers all have their own style, so make sure the images you are viewing are compatible with your own aesthetic. It is also important to be realistic about your expectations. The photographer can only capture what is available. Don't expect to have a shot like the one you saw of an outgoing bride and groom laughing and dancing if you know you are shy and uncomfortable on the dance floor.

When possible, it is a good idea to hire a photographer and videographer from the same company. This will ensure that the two professionals work together to capture seamless coverage of your wedding. It is not uncommon for a photographer and videographer to compete for shots or to set up shots the other has already taken. This leads to wasted time. If it is not possible to hire both from the same company, ask your photographer to recommend a videographer, or vice versa.

INNOVATIONS IN PHOTOGRAPHY

Digital photography is instantaneous. That's what we all love about it. The days of anxiously waiting for a photographer to develop your film are gone. In fact, these days many couples get a first glimpse on the actual day of their wedding.

Speak to your photographer about the different ways you could incorporate images from the ceremony into the reception. I recently planned a wedding where we displayed the wedding albums and post-ceremony portraits of the newlyweds' parents. Not wanting the bride and groom to be left out, we had the photographer bring a frame and board to the event so that immediately following the ceremony a formal portrait could be taken, printed by an assistant, framed, and then included in the display at the reception. The guests loved it. I've also seen brides feature an image of the ceremony kiss or the recessional propped on an easel at the reception's entrance. Another option is to present a slide show featuring images from the ceremony. This will be the first time the bride and groom are able to see what all their guests witnessed just hours before. The result is often emotional.

In recent years, the popularity of video montages has escalated. This is a photo compilation of the bride's and groom's lives, often from birth to their engagement photo. All images are scanned, put to music, and the final product is shown during the rehearsal dinner. It is not uncommon to have it playing at the reception as well, either during the cocktail hour or later in the evening near the bar.

if you're getting hitched abroad...

Your wedding might be on a tropical island, but I still suggest hiring a photographer whose studio is located in the city where you live. Most of your dealings with a photographer occur after the event, and it's much easier working with someone nearby. Plus, if you're throwing a local reception after the wedding, this same photographer might offer you a package deal to shoot both events. You should consider the expense of travel for your photographer as well as their accommodations and perhaps a daily per diem to cover their expenses while in the event city or country.

questions to ask the photographer and videographer

• **What is the cost of overtime on the day of the wedding?** Most photographers will allocate a set number of hours to shoot your wedding. This typically begins with the first click of their camera and ends with the last. Most will count the whole stretch of time, even if there is a three-hour delay in between the ceremony and reception.
• **What is the cost to add albums after the event?** Typically there is a charge for the first album and then a lesser charge for duplicates.
• **What is the charge to frame the portrait included in my package?** Charges vary depending on the type of frame, matting, and glass.
• **Can my guests order my wedding photos online? Is there an extra fee for this service?** Many photographers don't charge for this because it has taken the place of traditional proofs and is actually less expensive for them to produce.

AVOID HIDDEN CHARGES

Never assume a service is included just because you talked about it. Make certain every item is detailed on your contract. Specify the number of albums the photographer will provide, the size of the albums, the number of images they will include, the dimensions of the wedding portrait, the cost of sitting fees, and the length of time you will require a photographer on the day of the event. Ask whether you will own the images on disc and whether their resolution will be high enough for you to make your own prints. It is also not uncommon for a photographer to provide framing for portraiture. However, don't assume the cost of framing is included—it never is.

more questions to ask the photographer and videographer

• **What are the rates given to guests who wish to order prints?** Consider purchasing wallet-size photos for your thank-you cards.

• **What is the cost of enlarging a portrait?** Request a price list for portraiture extras.

• **Are you the photographer that will shoot my wedding or will you assign an assistant?**

• **Do you shoot color and black and white? Is there a charge for both?** There should be no extra charge.

• **How many photographers will be at my wedding?**

• **How much would it cost to have a second or third shooter?** Most photographers will charge a fee per shooter per segment. Segments range from one-hour to four-hour slots.

• **Do you have custom packages?** Photographers should allow you to tailor a package to suit your needs. Do not purchase a package with items that you do not want.

• **How long will it take after the wedding to receive my proofs?** It should never take longer than three weeks.

• **Do you offer complimentary photo retouching?** The better photographers do retouching. Others may charge a nominal fee.

• **Do your packages include a bridal portrait or engagement shoots?** Consider negotiating these items when purchasing a plan.

C ENTERTAINMENT

CHAPTER TWELVE *entertainment*

Every couple wants their guests to have a wonderful time. Hiring great entertainment is one way to ensure that happens. Music and dancing make a wedding feel like a celebration. Consider what type of music your guests enjoy and pick a band or disc jockey whose personality complements your event.

THE CEREMONY

Guests should be entertained from the moment they enter your ceremony venue until the time they depart. Entertainment agencies are an invaluable resource for local talent, and, for church weddings, you may find that your parish can provide a list of past performers.

An organist or pianist is a classic musical accompaniment to any church ceremony. You might also consider booking a harpist, bagpiper, string quartet, classical guitarist, trumpeters, or even a spirited gospel choir.

Couples not exchanging vows in a church will have far fewer restrictions. A band hired for a reception might also happily play a few processional and recessional tunes at the ceremony, or your DJ could provide the audio. Entertainment carry-overs, which involve the band or disc jockey wiring speakers into more than one room, is one way to get the most for your money.

THE RECEPTION

Use music to set the mood. If you want a quiet, elegant affair, consider a jazz ensemble or a DJ with a play list of strictly pop standards. If you want to bring down the house, a rock band or a DJ is an appropriate choice. If you hire a band, burn a CD of music to play during breaks to maintain the party's momentum. DJs require fewer breaks, so there is no need for you to contribute music beyond a play list. For an extra lively reception, hire both a band and a DJ. During band breaks, a DJ will take over seamlessly to keep the energy level high.

I often contract entertainment to fulfill a wedding's theme. For Old Hollywood Glam, I've called upon celebrity impersonators like Marilyn Monroe, Rock Hudson, Elizabeth Taylor, and even Andy Warhol. There are singers who impersonate Frank Sinatra, Harry Connick Jr., and all the famous crooners, as well as bands that play only big band classics or swing. I've even booked a henna artist and a tarot card reader for a wedding uniting a Hindu groom and a Southern belle bride. Don't be afraid to do something unique.

KEEP IT LIVELY

Besides musical entertainment, many receptions include a game or two. These are commonly led by the master of ceremonies or disc jockey and played after the toasts to liven up the crowd and get guests on the dance floor. Just be careful not to play too many. The following are two games that I often do at my weddings.

the newlywed game

To start, place the bride and groom in chairs back to back and hand each a bottle of beer and a glass of champagne. The master of ceremonies then asks the couple a series of questions, such as "Who is the best kisser?" or "Who is most likely to leave a trail of clothes from the front door to a favorite chair after work?" The bride and groom, without being able to see each other, holds up one of their drinks—the beer if the answer is the groom and the champagne if it is the bride. At times, the couple may hold up both drinks to prevent any hurt feelings. The whole scene is rather entertaining and an easy way to add some laughter to the evening.

the wedding top ten

This game is similar to David Letterman's Top Ten. During the cocktail hour, the master of ceremonies hands each guest a card inscribed with the question "Why are [bride's name] and [groom's name] so perfect together?" The guests write their answers on their cards. A few members of the bridal party collect them, read through them, and select the top ten best responses. We generally don't use the serious ones. Mostly we use the funny and slightly embarrassing ones. In the case of an inside joke, you may have to share a little background information for the entire room to get it. I once had a game where the bride's name was Liz and the No. 1 reason why she and the groom were a perfect pair was "because Liz said so." It was hilarious because Liz liked to have things her way and everyone knew it.

work the crowd

Your reception will need a master of ceremonies. Many DJs and bands will provide this service for you as a part of their contract. I often perform this role at my events; however, many wedding planners feel more comfortable staying behind the scenes. When selecting an emcee, avoid people who love the sound of their own voice. You don't want your entire wedding reception to be curtailed by someone talking all evening. Before the event, have a discussion with your master of ceremonies and make clear what components you want included and how much time should be spent making announcements.

prevent embarrassing moments

Not long ago I planned a wedding with a variety band. During the reception announcements, a cousin of the bride jumped up on stage and took a microphone for an unplanned and extremely unexpected announcement. She told the guests how happy she was to be at the wedding even though she had not been invited. She then went on to stun the crowd by telling everyone she was a lesbian. Learn from this couple's mistake—don't let just any guest take the stage, and make it clear with the band, master of ceremonies, and wedding planner exactly who can have access to the microphone.

SET THE PARTY TO MUSIC

As the evening goes on, it's not the stunning décor or the amazing dinner that keeps guests partying into the night—it's the music. Don't underestimate its importance. Consider the following options when deciding the soundtrack of your big day.

TYPES OF MUSIC

- Ambient
- Contemporary
- Country
- Disco
- Electronica
- Latin
- New age
- Pop and dance music from a specific decade
- Rockabilly
- Techno and world

TYPES OF BANDS

- Acoustic
- Alternative
- Americana
- Big band
- Bluegrass
- Blues
- Brass band
- Chamber music
- Christian
- Classic rock
- Classical ensemble
- Cover band
- Dixieland band
- Doo-wop
- Dueling pianos
- Easy listening
- Folk
- Funk
- Gospel
- Hard-core band
- Heavy metal
- Hip-hop
- Jazz
- Motown
- Oldies
- Party or variety band (most popular option)
- Pop
- Punk
- R&B
- Rap
- Reggae
- Rock
- Soul
- Southern rock
- Steel-drum band
- Swing
- Tribute band
- Vocal group
- Wedding band

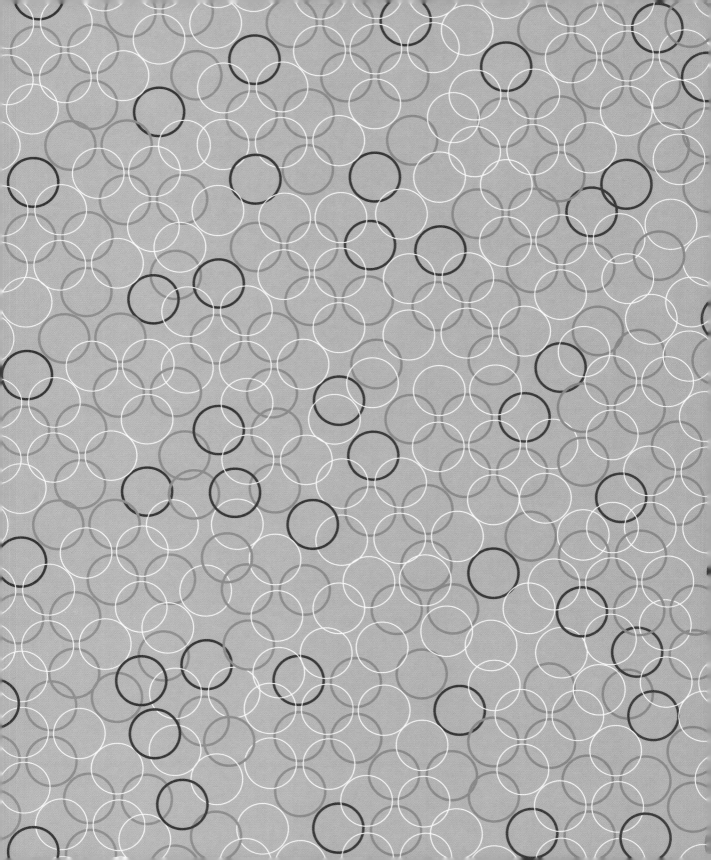

13

CHAPTER
TRANSPORTATION

CHAPTER THIRTEEN *transportation*

If you imagine yourself driving away in an antique Bentley or Hummer limo, make reservations early. Transportation is too often an afterthought, and as with any wedding vendor, availability is limited.

Whether it's a getaway mobile for you and your groom or shuttles to transport guests from the reception to a hotel, book transportation two to four months in advance. Keep in mind that rentals are in high demand during major holidays, the local high school's homecoming and prom, and the months of peak wedding season (March through June). Couples with weddings that fall within these dates will find themselves in a crunch if they wait to make arrangements a few weeks before their event. If you are forced to rent vehicles from a company in a nearby city, you'll not only have to pay the standard fee but also regional transfer costs, which can range from $100 to as much as $1,000. Don't procrastinate.

questions to ask a limousine company

• **How many, what size, and what type of vehicles do you carry?** Make sure they are not limited to one or two cars. You want them to have backup options in the event that the vehicle you've rented breaks down the day before your event.

• **Do you carry adequate insurance?**

• **Do you have commercial or limousine permits that allow you to park in a reserved area near our event?** This should go without saying.

• **What if you have car trouble or cannot be at my location on time?**

• **Do you have an hourly minimum?** There is usually a four- or six-hour minimum.

• **What is your policy for transfers? Can I do this instead of reserving the vehicle for the whole evening?** Transfers are when a driver picks up passengers, takes them to their destination, and then promptly leaves. A company's willingness to do transfers will depend on the season, day of the week, and time of day.

• **Do you provide refreshments in the car? If so, is there an extra charge for this?** Most companies do offer refreshments. Make sure the car is stocked with what you want. If they do not typically provide what you are requesting, ask them if they will provide the item for an extra charge or allow you to provide it in advance.

• **If our event is running late, will that create a problem for you?** Events frequently run late, and you should be aware of potential schedule conflicts.

• **Do you offer a complimentary red carpet for us to walk on?** This is a nice perk, but one that is only offered by nicer companies.

• **What are your payment terms and cancellation policy?**

• **Do you take credit cards?**

• **Is gratuity included in the fee?**

ACCOMMODATING GUESTS

Couples with a lengthy list of out-of-town guests ought to consider how these friends and family will get around during the wedding weekend.

Prearranging group transportation is one way a couple can relieve some of the stress of traveling. Even if guests rent cars, they probably aren't familiar with the city and may have difficulty finding the wedding venue. You may want to hire a shuttle to bring out-of-town guests and the wedding party from the hotel to the rehearsal dinner and then back to the hotel after the event. Similar transportation can also be provided from the hotel to the wedding ceremony, from the ceremony to the reception (if at an alternate location), and then from the reception back to the hotel. If guests are relying on a shuttle to return to the hotel, these vehicles must be available all evening. Not every guest will want to leave in the last hour, and you should accommodate any guest who wishes to turn in early.

You'll also want to consider transportation options when negotiating your room blocks. Many hotels will offer complimentary hotel-to-airport transfers. This is not always the case, but you should ask when booking your venue. Your guests will appreciate the courtesy.

THE GETAWAY MOBILE

It's become quite in vogue for the bride and groom to make their exit in a memorable vehicle. It's also a great photo op.

There are countless options, from horse-drawn carriages to tandem bicycles to vintage Harleys with sidecars. You might ask the hotel if they have a house limousine that can be used as part of your package. Perhaps a send-off in a Lamborghini or a Jaguar convertible is more your style. If you opt not to hire a driver, it's important to keep in check the number of drinks you consume at the reception. Do not spend your first night of married life in jail!

Limousine and party bus companies require customers to rent vehicles for a minimum number of hours. Sometimes you can get transfers for an inexpensive rate, but usually only during off-peak times. For a Saturday night, you are looking at a minimum requirement between four and eight hours. Read the fine print and make sure you understand the limousine minimums as well as the per hour charges. Ask if tax and gratuity are included, as well as tolls or other miscellaneous charges. I suggest paying these fees in advance so you don't have to think about them on the wedding day.

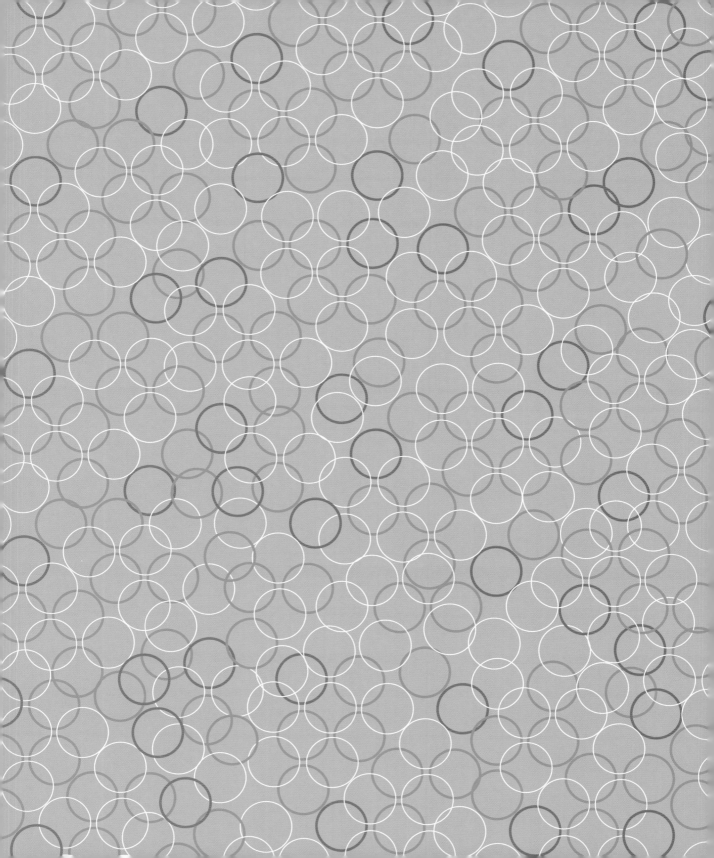

CHAPTER
ACCOMMODATIONS

14

CHAPTER FOURTEEN *accommodations*

In many cases, guests travel long distances to attend the weddings of family and friends. It's customary that couples arrange accommodations for these out-of-town guests, as well as for those who live nearby but would prefer the convenience of staying at a hotel. You don't have to pay for their rooms, but you should reserve space at a hotel. If you've chosen a resort as your wedding venue or if you can simply promise that your party will book a significant number of rooms, many establishments will roll out the red carpet.

GET THE BEST PRICE

It's no secret that buying in bulk is often cheaper—hotel rooms are no exception. Most hotels will offer you and your guests a special rate if you request a "room block."

Before calling the hotel, assemble some idea of how many guest rooms are needed for every night of the wedding weekend. Talk to your guests about their plans. If you have friends and family traveling in on Wednesday and the last leaving on Monday, you will need to set up a room block spanning from Wednesday through Sunday night. Be prepared to provide the hotel's sales manager with an estimated count for each night. Once a room block is secured, notify guests that there is a discount for those attending your wedding and instruct them to ask for the special rate when booking a room. This can easily be done on your save-the-date cards or your wedding Web site. You can also add an accommodations card to your main invitation. Typically, hotels will honor the discount for thirty or sixty days prior to the wedding date, so make sure you tell guests well in advance that the special rate is only available for a limited time period.

Every hotel chain has different rules pertaining to holding rooms in a block. Make sure you know how long the hotel will hold them, if you are responsible for unused rooms, and whether last-minute guests will have difficulty booking a room after the block expires. It's not uncommon for those who miss the room block to pay drastically higher rates or, worse, find that the hotel no longer has available rooms. Hotel rooms with no secure block are reserved much like airline tickets. The rates are flexible, but as demand increases so does the price. Read the fine print on your contract and keep asking questions until you thoroughly understand the hotel's policies.

There are perks to hosting a wedding reception at a hotel. When booking the venue, try to negotiate complimentary rooms for the newlywed couple, as well as the bride and groom's parents. When spending so much money at one establishment, you can often get a couple of rooms at no additional charge. Be sure to follow up on this type of agreement, as these reservations are usually made by the catering staff and can get overlooked by the reservations or room sales department.

THE WEDDING NIGHT SUITE

Most hotels offer romance packages that are either included in the price of the suite or available for an additional fee. While champagne and chocolate-covered strawberries are standard, some high-end hotels will even provide custom embroidered pillowcases with the couple's wedding logo.

You might consider asking your decorator or wedding planner to add a few decorative details to the suite. If you are leaving this job to members of your wedding party make sure they know to leave the silly string and "naughty" gag gifts at home, unless that is really what you want. The décor should be simple but romantic. Make sure the room's lighting is set perfectly. Check the lamps, the wall sconces, etc. Don't leave the room in darkness or with every light turned on. Below are several ways to create the perfect finish to a memorable day:

• A rose petal trail from the door to the bed or the bath or to a bottle of champagne on the suite's balcony
• A heart made of rose petals on the bed, perhaps with the couple's initials in the center
• Lit votive candles throughout the room
• A bubble bath drawn shortly before the couple arrives with orchid blooms resting on the bubbles and a bottle of champagne on ice next to the tub
• Two luxurious bathrobes monogrammed with the couple's initials
• A fruit and cheese plate with fresh breads
• If there is a gas fireplace in the room, turn it on low
• Two slices of wedding cake on a silver tray
• Florals from the reception, the ceremony, or a new arrangement
• A honeymoon gift basket decorated with ribbon and fabric and filled with thoughtful things: fragrant bath salts, a gas card (if the couple is driving to their destination), a gift certificate for two massages at the honeymoon resort, bottled waters, etc.

drunk rooms

It's inevitable that some of your friends and family will have one too many cocktails. To keep tipsy guests from driving, consider reserving and pre-paying for a few additional rooms at your hotel.

questions to ask a hotel about guest room accommodations

• **Do you have special room-block rates?** Most hotels will offer a block of rooms at a discounted rate for a specific amount of time.
• **What is your policy before and after the block release date?** Beware of contracts with an attrition clause, which allows a hotel to charge to your credit card any rooms that your guests do not reserve and the hotel does not sell after your room block expires. I advise negotiating a room block contract that won't make you pay for rooms you do not use.
• **If we have last-minute guests, will the hotel guarantee the original block rate?** Most hotels will not offer the discount after the block's expiration date.
• **Can my guests make their reservations directly with the hotel or do we have to make one large reservation?** Most hotels will give you a code for guests to use to ensure they get the special rate.
• **Are criminal background checks and drug tests performed on every employee?** This should be standard with most hotel chains.
• **Is there a fee to deliver welcome gifts to the guests' rooms before their arrival?** A fee is standard but should be affordable.
• **Does the hotel have non-smoking rooms?** Be kind to your non-smoking guests.
• **Are guest rooms equipped with safes? If so, is it large enough to secure a laptop?**
• **Do you offer complimentary airport transfers?** This can be negotiated with the hotel at the time of contracting.

EVENT INSURANCE

As the host of the party, you are responsible if guests drink and then drive. Obviously you cannot control what happens once a guest leaves the reception. Anything can happen. The last thing you want is for the alcoholic beverages you serve at your lavish affair to cause a tragedy.

I advise my clients to purchase event insurance. Many companies carry it. Perhaps your homeowner's policy offers coverage to protect you. Regardless, there are companies out there that specialize in this type of policy. WedSafe (www.wedsafe.com) has a variety of event-related packages to choose from, including liability packages that legally protect you if an intoxicated guest leaves your event and is injured or, God forbid, killed in an accident. Ordinarily, you would be named in the lawsuit along with the venue that served the alcohol. The venue has insurance to protect them, but this coverage does not cover you and your family. Event insurance plans are relatively inexpensive and, when you consider the stress relief involved, are very worthwhile.

These companies also have packages that cover other expenses if, for instance, your photographer's camera should fall into a pool at the hotel venue. With the right plan, they will pay to re-create the entire ceremony set for photography purposes. They will pay for new flowers, airline tickets for out-of-town family members, tuxedo rentals, and everything needed to reproduce and reshoot the valuable lost images that you are counting on to remember your wedding by.

When you are developing your budget, do yourself a favor and check into this type of insurance. You will be very happy you did.

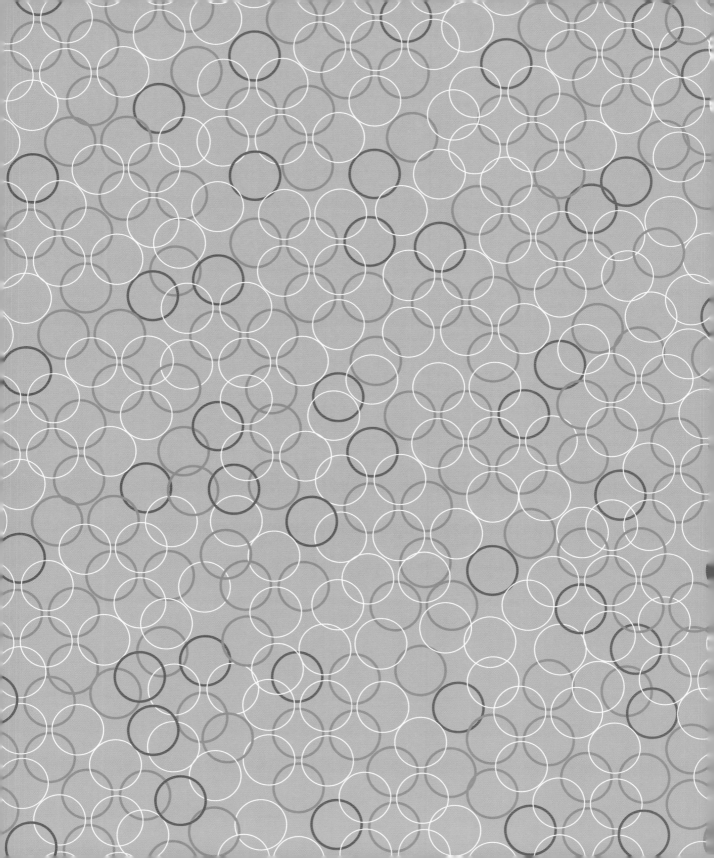

15

PRINTED MATERIALS

CHAPTER FIFTEEN *printed materials*

A beautiful wedding is like a good brand. Every element should seamlessly convey one concept or theme. Your printed materials are not only functional; they're also an opportunity to set a specific tone for your event. From the invitation sent months before the wedding to the thank-you note sent after the honeymoon, each printed item leaves an impression on guests and becomes a token of the celebration.

SAVE-THE-DATE CARDS

Save-the-date invitations are a relatively new concept. Couples mail them well in advance, sometimes as early as a year prior to the wedding, to prevent friends and family from making plans that will conflict with their date.

These early notices don't have to follow the wedding's theme or color palette. More often a reflection of the couple's humor and personality, save-the-date cards are a refreshing departure from the formal invitation and come in a variety of creative formats, including postcards and magnets. Even if you're planning a black-tie affair, don't be afraid to have a little fun with your save-the-date card. One of my all-time favorites told the story of how the engaged couple first met. The groom was a small town police officer; the bride had run a red light. The two met when he pulled her over. The save-the-date card had a photo of the groom in his police uniform standing outside the bride's car issuing her a ticket. The image was hilarious and a topic of conversation at the wedding.

SELECTING INVITATIONS

The invitation is a guest's first impression of a wedding. It should do more than merely outline the day's events, specify how guests should dress, and provide details on dates, times, and locations. Of course providing all this information is essential, but a proper invitation also gives other clues about the upcoming event. The paper stock, color palette, graphics, and the overall formality of the fonts and wording should all accurately match the personality of the wedding. If it's done well, guests should know all they need to know upon reading their invitations.

As you shop, you'll be amazed at the diversity of styles, colors, and formats. Wedding boutiques and stationery shops will have sample books that you can browse through. Their associates can provide cost quotes and walk you through the ordering process. There are also independent wedding invitation designers who can custom design a whole line of printed materials for your special occasion. If you have designed a personal logo for your wedding, consider incorporating it on custom invitations or stationery.

MAILING INVITATIONS

Always thoughtfully package your invitations before dropping them in the mail. Usually the following items are tucked inside an envelope and then placed into an outer envelope that prevents the contents from arriving damaged:

• The main invitation, the most stately item within the envelope, provides the date, time, and location of the ceremony.

• The reception card outlines the date, time, and location of the reception. It should also specify the type of dinner that will be served, as well as details about the cocktail hour, if there is one.

• The RSVP card gives guests a way to formally accept or decline. If guests have their choice of a main entrée at the reception, include the menu options on the RSVP card so that you can share entrée preferences with the caterer. The RSVP card should have its own return envelope that is pre-stamped and pre-addressed. If you are inviting a number of underage people, you might also ask for the number of adults and the number of adolescents attending. This will give you an accurate count for children's meals as well as an estimate on the number of guests who will consume alcohol.

• The rehearsal dinner invitation can either be mailed with the wedding invitation or sent separately. Remember that not everyone on your guest list is invited to the rehearsal dinner, so be careful not to send an invitation to someone who should not receive one. Only the wedding party, immediate family, and out-of-town guests should be included.

Mail invitations a little more than two months prior to the wedding and specify a thirty-day deadline on the RSVP card. Some planners say that requesting guests to RSVP two weeks before the event is plenty of time, but I often find that many guests respond a week or two late. You don't want to be caught without a final head count when it's time to submit one to your floral designer and caterer. Most caterers or in-house dining establishments want a final head count at least seven days prior to the event. (To minimize confusion, I always suggest that my clients provide the guest count both verbally and in writing.) If you miss your deadline, you must pay for the maximum number of meals guaranteed by your contract. If the guest count is higher than anticipated, you might not have enough food at your reception. Some caterers will automatically cook for 5–10 percent more guests than expected with no financial penalties unless they have to serve the extra food. This is not a standard practice, so ask your catering manager about the company's policy in advance.

questions to ask the invitation designer or sales associate

• **How long have you worked in the wedding business?**

• **Do you offer complimentary proofs? If so, how many? What if we decide to make changes along the way?** Most companies provide two complimentary proofs; beyond that, they charge a fee.

• **Will the final product look exactly like the proofs?** Only place orders with companies that answer "yes" to this question. Do not allow them to go to press before you have carefully reviewed the proofs and signed off on them.

• **Do you hand make the invitations or are they purchased from a company that mass produces them?** Make sure you are getting the invitations you want, even if that means paying more and purchasing handmade or custom invitations.

• **Do you offer envelope calligraphy?** If they don't, ask if they can offer a good referral.

• **Do you design and print other wedding-related materials (thank-you cards, programs, menu cards, etc.)?**

• **What is your payment and cancellation policy?**

• **Do you accept credit cards or personal checks?**

• **Can I receive the envelopes in advance?** This enables you to have a calligrapher address your envelopes while the invitations and enclosures are at the printer.

GIFT ENCLOSURE CARDS

Typically couples include thoughtful notes with the gifts that they leave in their guests' hotel rooms. They might also provide additional event information and a list of favorite nearby restaurants and city sights that guests may enjoy during their stay.

To further carry the theme of your wedding, coordinate these cards with the rest of your printed wedding materials.

PROGRAMS

The program outlines the ceremony. It lists each component of the service, states who is involved in each event, and instructs guests when to stand, kneel, or sing. Like any printed material, it too can easily reinforce the wedding's theme and provide guests with something to read while waiting for the event to begin. Programs generally consist of the following components:

- The ceremony itinerary
- Musical selections, in chronological order
- Reading selections, in chronological order
- Names of the wedding party, including the parents, grandparents, honor attendants, attendants, ushers, and house party
- Names of additional important participants—readers, singers, the officiant, musicians, the wedding planner, etc.
- The time and location of any post-ceremony events, such as a cocktail hour and dinner reception

The Wedding Ceremony
Uniting

Christine Ann Carman

and

Allen Reid Stiles

Saturday, November 18, 2006
The Chapel at Christ Church
Plano, Texas

MAPS AND DIRECTIONS

These are necessary if there is travel between events and guests need information such as parking, shortcuts, etc. You can include these in the main invitation or hand them out at the ceremony with the program. Ask your reception facility if they have a map you can reproduce for this purpose.

PLACE CARDS AND ESCORT CARDS

Place cards are generally used for seated dinners and indicate where each guest should sit. I'm not an advocate of place cards because they create the challenge of having to decide who sits next to whom.

Today, most wedding planners use escort cards instead. These are typically folded cards that assign guests to a table, not a specific chair. Generally the guests' names appear on the front with the table's name or number printed inside. The cards are displayed in alphabetical order on a table directly outside the reception area so that guests can easily pick them up as they arrive. Escort cards are far less hassle than place cards, and your guests will appreciate the flexibility of choosing their own seats.

MENU CARDS

A menu card is only necessary if you are having a seated dinner. They enable guests to alert the catering staff in advance if they are vegetarian, kosher, or allergic to specific foods. Most caterers plan five to ten vegetarian plates for every wedding. Make sure you ask what that would consist of at your tasting. Besides their functional purpose, menu cards also serve as a decorative element, beautifully carrying the wedding theme to the table.

THANK-YOU CARDS

If the invitation is the first impression, the thank-you card is the last. It is the final item given to your wedding guests, usually four to six weeks after the event. As with the invitation, these cards should echo the concept and tone of your wedding celebration. Purchase them with the rest of your printed materials, and order a couple dozen extra to carry you into the first year of marriage.

FANCY SCRIPT

Calligraphy is rarely seen on every element of a wedding invitation. The sheer variety of specialty invitations on the market, not to mention the incredible expense associated with hand lettering, has dramatically affected calligraphy's popularity.

Regardless of whether you order preprinted or custom-printed invitations, you may still want to have the inner and outer envelopes engraved with calligraphy. An elegantly handwritten address stands out amongst mounds of everyday mail and immediately signifies to recipients that they are about to open something special.

When hiring a calligrapher, examine their samples, ask about pricing, and discuss how much time it will take to complete and deliver the work. Don't skimp on this vendor. You need a professional who can do a flawless job. Incorrectly addressing an envelope could preclude important guests from receiving their invitations. Prices will vary from $1.25 per line to $3 and up. I am not a fan of couples addressing their envelopes themselves. The polished look that calligraphy gives a wedding invitation is worth the expense.

the look for less

Even a time-honored craft can get a digital makeover. Instead of hiring a calligrapher, you might consider having your calligraphy applied by a machine. There are a number of companies offering this service. They simply type the wording of your invitation or guest's names and addresses for envelopes into a computer spreadsheet, set the type style and parameters, and insert a special calligraphic pen into a device. The pen will write on whatever card stock is used. This electronic method isn't labor intensive and costs at least 50 percent less than a traditional calligrapher.

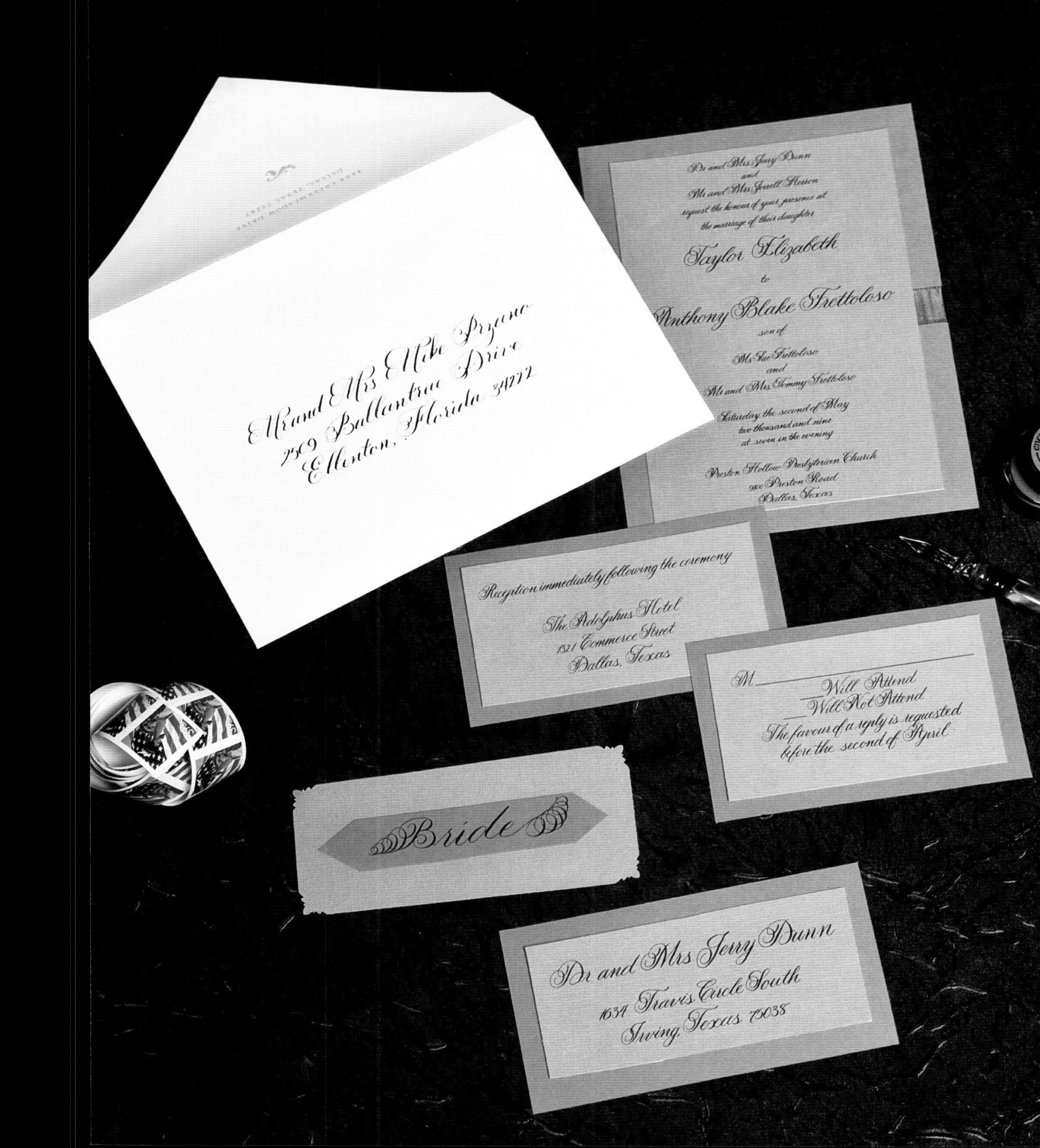

Dr and Mrs Jerry Dunn
and
Mr and Mrs Jewell Flerien
request the honour of your presence at
the marriage of their daughter

Taylor Elizabeth

to

Anthony Blake Frettoloso

son of

Ms Sue Frettoloso
and
Mr and Mrs Tommy Frettoloso

Saturday, the second of May
two thousand and nine
at seven in the evening

Preston Hollow Presbyterian Church
980 Preston Road
Dallas, Texas

Mr and Mrs E Mike Przano
2509 Ballantrae Drive
Ellenton, Florida 34222

Reception immediately following the ceremony

The Adolphus Hotel
1521 Commerce Street
Dallas, Texas

M _____ Will Attend
_____ Will Not Attend
The favour of a reply is requested
before the second of April

Bride

Dr and Mrs Jerry Dunn
1634 Travis Circle South
Irving, Texas 75038

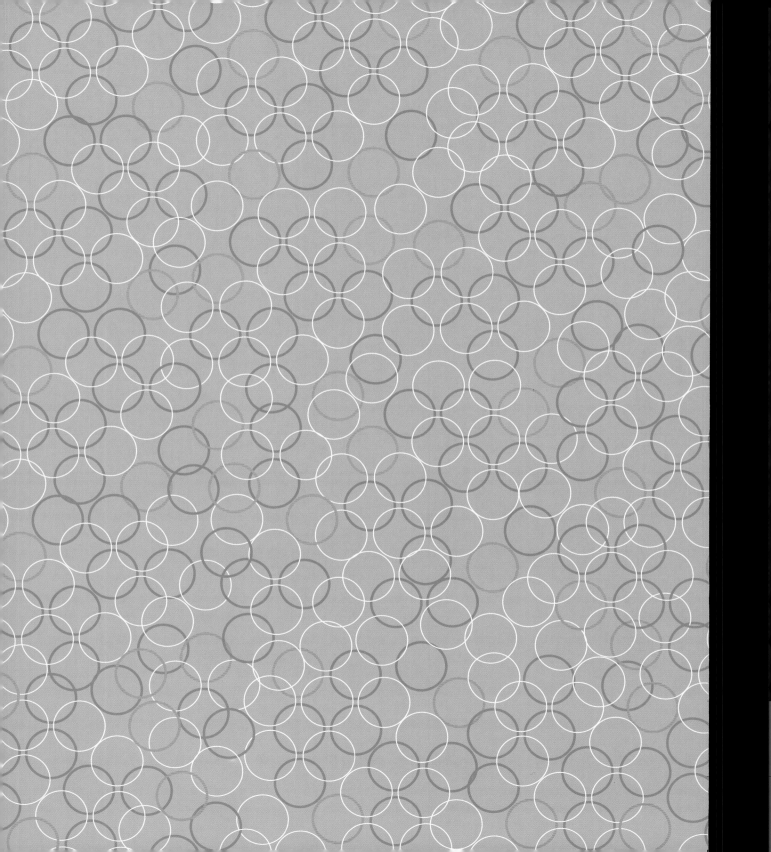

FINAL
PREPARATIONS

16

CHAPTER SIXTEEN *final preparations*

The days before a wedding are often filled with welcome parties, golf outings, family dinners, and any number of activities that the local area has to offer. At this stage, you have hired your professionals, negotiated their contracts, and followed up with each vendor. Sit back and let your wedding professionals do what they do best. It is now time for you to simply enjoy yourself.

THE REHEARSAL

The best way to ensure that your ceremony goes smoothly is to practice. The rehearsal is generally held the day before the wedding. I recommend scheduling rehearsals around the same time of day that you will hold the actual ceremony. Not only does this give you a preview of the location's lighting; it also helps everyone mentally register exactly where and when they need to arrive.

Rehearsals are not optional. Everyone who has a role in the ceremony needs to attend, from the ushers and the house party to the attendants and anyone being formally seated during the ceremony. If a groomsman lives in another country, he will need to fly in a day early to participate in the run-through. No exceptions. Your entire celebration will look disorganized if these key friends and family members don't know exactly when to proceed down the aisle, whom they're escorting, or where to stand.

If you hired a wedding planner, he or she should be on hand. Meet with your planner in advance to discuss how you want the ceremony conducted. If there is a church coordinator, the wedding planner and coordinator should also meet beforehand to share notes. At the rehearsal, your planner and/or coordinator will provide instruction on how to proceed during the processional and recessional, your officiant will walk everyone through the ceremony, and you should be able to relax.

Organizing a crowd is always a challenge. Luckily you will have a wedding planner, church coordinator, and/or officiant to do this job for you. Regardless, you may find the following points helpful in keeping your rehearsal running smoothly:

• If there are small children in the processional; watch them closely and see whether they are able to stand in place on the altar for the length of time it takes the officiant to run through the ceremony. If they fidget, seat them after the processional instead and then move them back to the altar for the recessional.

• Another note about children is that the pace they walk down the aisle is unimportant. People understand that small children don't act like older adults. Let the children be children.

• If there are a few critical people in the wedding party who arrive late, don't wait to begin the rehearsal. Instead, ask some extra guests to stand in for those who are missing. These guests can then fill them in on what they missed.

STEP BY STEP

There are a number of ways to lead a rehearsal. I generally begin by positioning everyone on the altar or in their seats as though they have already walked down the aisle. After the couple and wedding party understand where to stand after the processional, we perform a mock recessional in order to practice leaving the altar. When that's finished, I line everyone up as though it is time to begin the ceremony. It's important that people remember whom they are between and beside. We then conduct a mock processional and land at the points on the altar or in the seats where we were positioned earlier. (If any family members or friends will be escorted to a seat during the processional, this should also be rehearsed.) Once everyone has gathered back on the altar, the officiant provides an overview of the ceremony. The last step is practicing the recessional one more time, without my assistance—they must know their cues, after all. I then typically conclude with a few announcements about timing, offer some final reminders, and release everyone to the rehearsal dinner.

practice makes perfect

A wedding ceremony is like a well-choreographed dance. Movements should be fluid and synchronized. If you want your ceremony to look flawless, practice these tips at the rehearsal:

• Bridesmaids and groomsmen should always stand with their bodies pointed entirely toward the bride. If they are standing in position at the altar and the bride has not yet walked down the aisle, they should face the doorway that she will walk through. As she moves past them, they should slowly pivot their bodies toward her. This is a fantastic way to create a well-rehearsed, beautiful ceremony.

• The bride and her bridesmaids should always hold their bouquets at navel level with their elbows slightly bent. Many ladies tend to hold their bouquets up toward their chins, which doesn't look as polished. Uniformity is key in a ceremony and bouquet height is one of the critical components in making this event look flawless.

• Unless a groomsman is escorting someone, he should stand with his hands left over right, in a fig leaf configuration.

THE REHEARSAL DINNER

The dinner held directly after the rehearsal is a special evening spent with those you love most. The past several months of planning probably felt like a whirlwind. Now that it's done, savor the moment. Visit with family and friends, and happily anticipate what the next day will bring.

Traditionally paid for by the groom's family, the rehearsal dinner is similar to a small-scale wedding reception. It can be as elaborate or as simple as you would like. Often these dinners pay tribute to the region in which the wedding is being held or celebrate the cultural heritage of the bride and groom. I have planned down-home barbeques, Italian family-style feasts, spreads of sushi, and Mexican fiestas.

Toasts are inevitable at rehearsal dinners. This may be the first opportunity for friends and family to get to know one another. Naturally, guests will want to share stories and express their happiness for the couple. You can either predetermine who will give toasts or you can open the microphone. Either way, brace yourself for potentially embarrassing anecdotes. If you fear that your speakers' content may be inappropriate, speak to them before the dinner to avoid hard feelings later. If the dinner location is spacious, you might consider renting audio equipment so that every guest can hear the toasts. Some facilities will have equipment available. If they don't, the venue can likely offer a referral, as can your videographer or DJ.

PRE-WEDDING BEAUTY SECRETS

An important part of getting ready for your big day is taking action to look and feel your best. I cannot stress enough the importance of a good night's sleep. A lack of rest can wreak havoc on your complexion. Try not to drink too much at your rehearsal dinner and get to bed early.

It is also essential to eat healthily in the days leading up to the big event. In my experience, "nervous jitters" aren't usually triggered by second thoughts on marriage. More often, they're your body's reaction to the past several months of intense stress, anxiety, and excitement. You can counter some of this by eating right, especially on your wedding day and the day before.

honeymoon prep

It's hard enough packing a suitcase for a big trip under normal circumstances. Your mind will be so cluttered the week of your wedding, it's inevitable that you'll forget something. The following is a checklist to ensure that you leave the house at least with the essentials.

☐ Cash
☐ Bottled water
☐ Cell phone with chargers
☐ Checks for any vendors that require final payments
☐ Contact information for family, friends, and wedding vendors
☐ Credit cards
☐ Driver's license and/or other photo ID
☐ Gifts for family, attendants, and fiancé
☐ Jewelry (any you will need for the wedding and honeymoon)
☐ Keys (for the car and house)
☐ Marriage license
☐ Medications (anything you might need)
☐ Packed suitcases for the honeymoon
☐ Passport (if needed for the honeymoon)
☐ Portable flashlight
☐ Shoes, an extra pair (plus flats for later in the evening, if desired)
☐ Snacks
☐ Sunglasses
☐ Sunscreen (depending on the season)
☐ Travel tickets
☐ Umbrella
☐ Watch

WEDDING-DAY EMERGENCY KIT

You would think that assembling your wedding-day emergency kit would be relatively simple. However, this is not a task to leave for the night before your big day. In the weeks leading up to your wedding, gradually gather the items listed below. Every wedding will have its own special requirements, but the following are necessities that no wedding-day emergency kit should be without:

- Baby powder (for all the reasons you can think of)
- Band-Aids (assorted)
- Cologne for the men
- Comb (tooth comb and a pick)
- Complete makeup kit (everything you could possibly need including base, powder, blush, eyeliner, mascara, lipstick, and gloss)
- Double-sided tape (for those pesky gown emergencies)
- Duct tape
- Emery board (maybe even a complete manicure kit)
- Evian Mist (to refresh yourself or assist in setting makeup)
- Extra earring backs
- Eyeglass cleaner and wipes (you can also get pre-moistened pads sealed in foil pouches)
- Hairbrush (a straight brush and a round brush)
- Hair curling iron
- Hair dryer (with diffuser)
- Hair elastics
- Hair styling products (including light-hold and heavy-hold hair spray; this can also be used to remove static cling from clothing)
- Hair pins (make sure they are the right color or have an assortment)
- Hair straightener
- Hand sanitizer
- Handkerchief (several)
- Hem tape (you never know)
- Iron (with linen napkins to protect delicate fabrics from high heat)
- Lint brush
- Mints or breath freshener
- Mirror (a small portable one so you can see the back of your head)
- Moist towelettes
- Mouthwash
- Needles and thread (thread colors should include matches for all the formal wear worn by the wedding party)
- Pain killers (aspirin and ibuprofen)
- Panty hose (several shades if needed)
- Perfume for the ladies
- Razor and shaving cream
- Safety pins (large and small)
- Scissors (small and large)
- Shoe polish (for all the shoe colors)
- Shoe-shine pad
- Smelling salts
- Spot remover (spot and bleach pens)
- Static cling spray
- Straight pins (corsage pins with the pearl on the end work well)
- Super Glue
- Tampons and pads
- Teeth-bleaching kit (personal or package of bleaching strips)
- Toothbrush (several in case they are needed after eating and before walking down the aisle)
- Toothpaste (whitening is best)

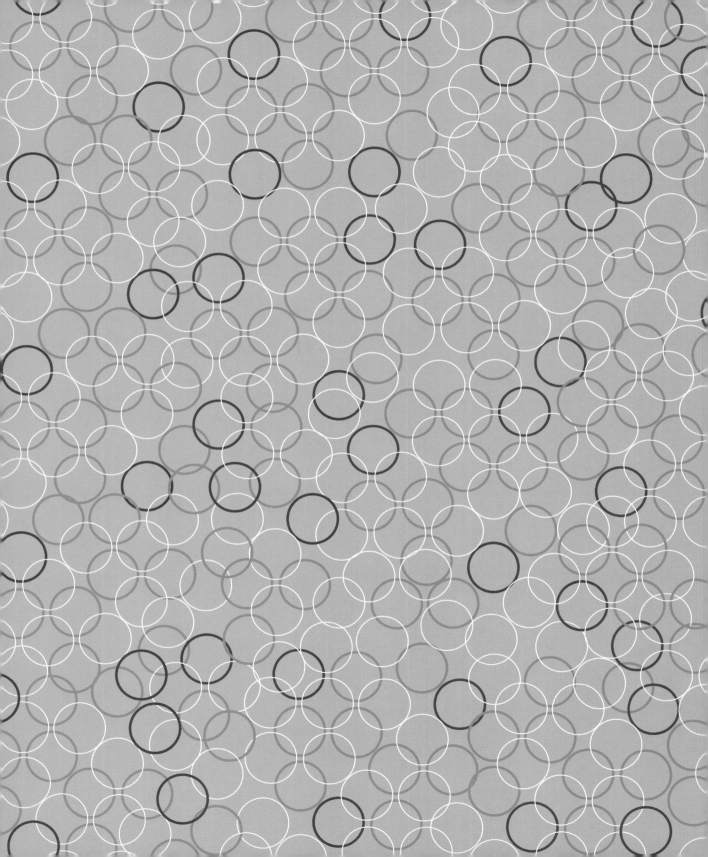

17

CHAPTER
THE BIG EVENT

CHAPTER SEVENTEEN *the big event*

Happy Wedding Day! This should be the most wonderful twenty-four hours of your entire life. Your guests are here. The plans are in place. Your vendors are booked and confirmed and reconfirmed. You've thought of every last detail. It's time to let go.

START YOUR DAY RIGHT

My first bit of advice is simple: eat breakfast. I know that this is your wedding day and you want your gown to fit, but you also don't want to pass out from lack of nourishment. A helping of protein or whole grains will prepare you for the long day ahead. Even the very happiest of brides at some point feel overwhelmed, stressed, scared, anxious, or jittery. Don't try to cope with this whirl of emotion on an empty stomach.

I also recommend padding your schedule. If you are holding a pre-wedding brunch or tea, schedule the event early in the day so that you don't feel rushed afterward. Nothing ever goes exactly as planned. Someone will arrive late or you'll forget something and need to turn the car around. Keep the stress level low by leaving yourself more than enough time.

On that note, you also don't want to get dressed too early. Schedule your dressing so that you will be ready for pre-ceremony photographs, but don't put on your dress hours before walking down the aisle. The longer you're in your gown the more time you have to spill something on yourself or wrinkle the fabric. Try not to sit down often and don't wear anything that will leave a noticeable mark on your skin, such as rings, necklaces, bracelets, bra straps, and watches. Allow time for red marks or impressions to disappear so that you look flawless.

Also, pardon me for getting personal, but wedding gowns are a bit cumbersome in the ladies room—another reason not to slip into them too soon. A bride should take her necessary bathroom break right before she steps into her gown. She will be able to go again after the dress is on, but not as easily.

PRE-CEREMONY PHOTOGRAPHY

It used to be considered bad luck for the groom to see the bride before the ceremony. Today, many couples ignore this tradition and do a portion of their wedding photography before the ceremony begins. If you are not seeing each other, you may still want to do some of your photography before the wedding with only those people who are allowed to see you. This way you will have less to shoot later. The last thing you want is for a lengthy session of post-ceremony photography to keep you from arriving to the reception on time.

HAIR AND MAKEUP

Scheduling hair and makeup appointments is logistically tricky. You must arrange them so that everyone is done around the same time and well in advance of the pre-ceremony photography.

Unless you have a makeup artist and hair stylist that you use regularly, it can be a challenge finding the right person for the job. Begin by researching the professional wedding hair and makeup artists in your area. They typically come to you so that you don't have to travel across town on your big day. Once you've found a good prospect, schedule a dry run so that you and the stylist can test different looks. You might consider using this person to do hair and makeup for the pre-wedding portrait or the engagement photo shoot. This is a great way to verify whether you can truly trust this stylist with your hair and makeup on your wedding day.

Do not ask a stylist to do your hair and then take a picture of the hairstyle to another stylist to recreate the day of the wedding; you are setting yourself up for disappointment. Also, these makeup and hair artists should be available to do other women in the wedding party. Photos are so much nicer when everyone is camera ready.

questions to ask a makeup artist and hair stylist

- **Do you do makeup or hair on-site or do I have to come to you?** You want to hire someone who will do a good job and make this process convenient.
- **Are there travel charges if you come to me?** Make sure that you are comfortable with these charges.
- **How many faces or heads of hair can you do for a wedding?** You do not want the stylist to be overworked or stressed out when working on you!
- **Do you have assistants to bring with you?** It is important that they have enough staff to do the job comfortably.
- **Do you offer a complimentary preview?** Most professionals do.
- **How long do you stay after makeup and/or hair is completed?** You may want a touch-up before the reception.
- **How do I keep my hair and makeup looking fresh throughout the entire day?** They are professionals and should be able to offer you several tips.
- **What products do you use?** Make sure they are using professional products and not those bought in drug stores.
- **Are you licensed by the state?** Never, ever use anyone who is not licensed or has an expired license.
- **Do you sell your products?** You may fall in love with a product and want to begin using it regularly.
- **What is your payment/cancellation policy?**
- **Do you accept credit cards?**
- **Do you use airbrush makeup techniques?**
- **Do you have a backup in case of emergency or illness?**
- **What are your fees?**

WALKING DOWN THE AISLE

The processional usually begins with a musical overture, which cues the wedding party to begin processing down the aisle. The following are two sample processionals. One involves the men escorting the women down the aisle and the other has the men filing in from the side of the altar. I've also included a sample recessional. Hopefully these ideas will help you decide how you want to approach and leave the altar.

processional one

- Grandmother(s) of the groom escorted by usher
- Followed by grandfather(s)
- Grandmother(s) of the bride escorted by usher
- Followed by grandfather(s)
- Mother of groom escorted by usher
- Followed by father of groom
- Mother of bride escorted by usher
- *Music change to processional*
- Attendant (farthest away from bride on altar) escorted by groomsman
- Attendant (next farthest from bride on altar) escorted by groomsman
- And so on ...
- Ring bearer
- Flower girl(s)
- *Music change to bridal processional*
- Bride escorted by father of bride or other escort

processional two

- Grandmother(s) of the groom escorted by usher
- Followed by grandfather(s)
- Grandmother(s) of the bride escorted by usher
- Followed by grandfather(s)
- Mother of groom escorted by usher
- Followed by father of groom
- Mother of bride escorted by usher
- *Music change to processional*
- Groom and groomsmen enter from the side of the altar
- Attendant(s)
- Ring bearer
- Flower girl(s)
- *Music change to bridal processional*
- Bride escorted by father of bride or other escort

recessional

- Bride and groom
- Flower girl(s)
- Ring bearer
- Best man and maid of honor
- Attendants with groomsmen
- Mother of bride escorted by father of bride
- Mother of groom escorted by father of groom
- Grandmother(s) of bride escorted by grandfather(s) or usher
- Grandmother(s) of groom escorted by grandfather(s) or usher

THE CEREMONY

The ceremony is really the reason behind the entire wedding celebration. Sometimes couples get so caught up in the rest of the event that they lose sight of the ceremony's importance. Take time to think this part out carefully and work with your officiant to ensure that the readings, music, and vows will hold meaning for you as a couple. Just as you personalize your reception, you should also create a ceremony that reflects your beliefs, values, and style. It is your wedding—not your mother's, not anyone else's. This is your time to have the event of your dreams.

GET THE PARTY STARTED

The reception generally begins with a cocktail hour, allowing guests to mingle as they wait for the bride and groom to arrive. Don't open the ballroom until the wedding party arrives. It is up to the couple whether they want to catch a glimpse of the reception room before it floods with guests. I like to work out the logistics so that this is possible. It gives the newlyweds a few moments of peace in the beautifully decorated room and lets them catch their breath before the party begins.

Many couples like to make a grand entrance with their wedding party. These introductions are a nice touch and a chance to pump excitement into the room. The newlyweds and their attendants ought to have some fun and work the crowd when their names are announced. As the groomsmen and bridesmaids enter the reception, have them form a half moon around the dance floor so that the couple will be partially encircled when they begin their first dance.

RECEPTION TIMING

Creating momentum is critical. Structure your evening like a great play. Every event should build on the next, without a lull in between. The grand finale should be your big send-off at the end of the night. If you pace your evening properly, most guests will forget about the time and stick around until the end.

I have listed below the traditional components of a wedding reception followed by some good advice. The reception timing is entirely up to you. Organize these events any way you wish. After all, this is your wedding reception and you should tailor it to your liking.

- Introductions
- Bride and groom's first dance
- Welcome
- Pre-dinner prayer
- Dinner
- Dancing
- Chicken dance (just kidding!)
- Cake cutting
- Toasts
- Games
- Father-daughter dance
- Mother-son dance
- Wedding party dance
- Hava Nagila (if Jewish)
- Dollar dance (I hate this tradition, but if you need tip money for your honeymoon, by all means!)
- General dancing
- Bouquet toss
- Garter toss
- Send-off

You do not have to include all of these things. I threw in the chicken dance to be funny. You can do it if you want, but I find it to be a bit trite.

the jitters

Many brides get a little queasy before walking down the aisle. I find humor gets the mind off the stomachache. It is always the best medicine. When you are selecting your wedding party, make sure you include that person in your life who always makes you laugh.

the stepfamily

What role should a stepmother or stepfather play in a wedding ceremony? I hear this question almost more than any other. The couple must decide what makes them feel most comfortable. Consider how close you are to them and proceed accordingly. Some couples choose to handle stepfamily and blood relatives in the same way, with the same flowers and positioning at the ceremony. In other situations, equal treatment would be inappropriate. Generally, stepparents walk behind the blood family in the processional. However, if you are not close at all, you can have them pre-seated in a place that does not make your blood family uncomfortable.

WEDDING DAY ITINERARY

When I say that I map out every minute of an event, I'm not exaggerating. I create an outline similar to the one you see below for each wedding. I recommend that you do the same. It's the best way to figure out how you want to organize and time your event.

7:00 AM Girls' breakfast in bride's suite

8:00 AM Bride and girls' hair and makeup

9:00 AM Men's breakfast in groom's suite

10:30 AM Reception décor installation begins

11:00 AM Décor installation at the ceremony site begins

11:30 AM Men's pre-ceremony photos at hotel lobby

11:55 AM Women's pre-ceremony photos with groom

12:10 PM Bride and girls arrive, pre-photos at hotel lobby

12:30 PM Men leave in limo for ceremony site from ballroom entry

12:45 PM Girls leave in limo from main lobby entry

12:55 PM Men arrive at ceremony site

1:10 PM Girls arrive at ceremony site

1:15 PM Family leaves in limo from hotel lobby entry

1:30 PM Guest arrival at ceremony site

1:40 PM Family arrives at ceremony site

1:55 PM Men line up for processional

1:55 PM Girls line up for processional

2:00 PM Processional begins

3:00 PM Band arrives for setup

3:00 PM Cake delivery

3:30 PM Recessional

3:40 PM Family post-ceremony photos

3:40 PM Guests leave for reception site

4:00 PM Ketubah signing (if Jewish)

4:10 PM Wedding party leaves for reception

5:00 PM Wedding party arrives at reception

5:30 PM Guests arrive at reception and cocktail hour on terrace begins

5:45 PM Reception décor setup complete

6:15 PM Dinner chimes and guests move to ballroom

6:30 PM Ballroom opens

6:50 PM Wedding party intros

7:05 PM First dance

7:10 PM Welcome by father of bride

7:13 PM Challah toast (if Jewish)

7:15 PM Dinner is served

8:30 PM Father-daughter dance

8:35 PM Mother-son dance

9:00 PM Cakes are cut

9:15 PM Toasts

9:30 PM Top ten game

9:35 PM Hava Nagila (if Jewish)

9:40 PM Dancing

11:00 PM Limousine arrives

11:20 PM Guests line up for send-off

11:30 PM Send-off

Event strike

THE FIRST DANCE

The bride and groom's first dance should be done at a time when they will have the room's full attention. I prefer to schedule it right after introductions. Not only does this guarantee that guests watch; it also eliminates the anticlimactic feeling that occurs when the newlyweds just take their seats after their big entrance.

To personalize the first dance, some couples prerecord sentimental messages to each other to play during the instrumental parts of their song. You can apply this same concept to the father-and-daughter dance or the mother-and-son dance. This is a touching way to ensure that your thoughts and emotions don't go unexpressed.

CUTTING THE CAKE

I generally cut the cake late in the evening. Delaying the cake cutting is one way to keep guests from leaving the reception early. I'm not suggesting that you wait hours, but an hour after dinner is perfectly acceptable.

TOASTING THE COUPLE

Make the toasts short and sweet. I once had a client who allowed two hours worth of toasting. That is the best way I know to lose an audience. I recommend limiting toasts to the fathers of the bride and groom, the best man, and the maid of honor. Let each person know beforehand how much time they can have at the microphone and attempt to keep the total toasting time to around fifteen minutes. Any longer and your guests will get restless.

BOUQUETS AND GARTERS

Keep the reception's energy level high by holding the traditional bouquet and garter toss toward the end of the night. Often, I advise the bride to fake the toss a couple of times in order to get the crowd going. For the garter, I always encourage the groom and his friends to have some fun with the toss. For instance, I recently had a groom who bought a pair of plus-size panties and stuffed them up his sleeves at the reception. When he went under his bride's gown to retrieve the garter, he pulled out the granny panties instead. The crowd went nuts. These are the types of things that make a memorable night.

THE SEND-OFF

More than a great photo opportunity, the grand send-off is a celebratory moment when the guests applaud the newlywed couple and express their best wishes. In the past, send-offs were held directly following the church ceremony, but these days most couples shoot their wedding photography after the ceremony and schedule their big send-off after the reception.

Even if you hold the send-off at the end of the night, that doesn't mean the fun has to stop. You can always make an announcement as the reception is winding down that guests are welcome to join the couple at the hotel or another establishment for a wedding after-party, often off the tab of the couple and their families.

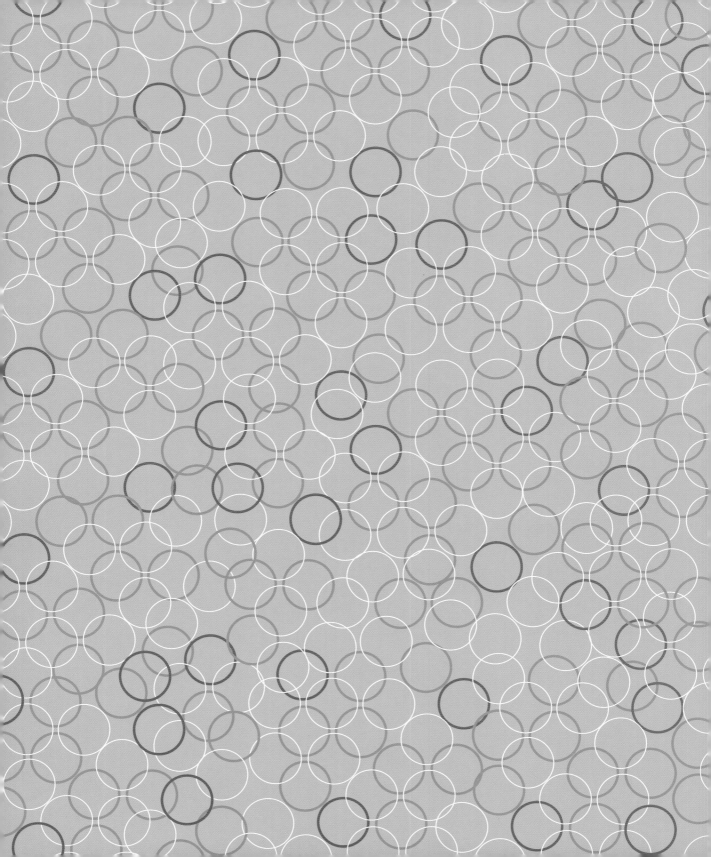

CHAPTER
THE HONEYMOON AND AFTERWARD

18

CHAPTER EIGHTEEN *the honeymoon and afterward*

The wedding is over. You are likely experiencing a calm feeling rush over you, along with perhaps some uneasiness about how much time and money you spent planning the wedding. Not to worry; this is normal. You don't have to move on to the next step just yet. There is still the honeymoon. And then, when you return, the beginning of a new chapter with the love of your life.

PLAN YOUR PERFECT TRIP

Wedding festivities usually begin with an engagement ring and finish with a honeymoon. Tropical resorts and cruises are such common destinations that they've become a tad cliché. While there is nothing wrong with either, know that there are countless other ways to spend a honeymoon. You might enjoy canoeing the Boundary Waters, going on an African safari, or skiing in the Alps. Whatever you decide, make sure you are both equally happy with the decision and that it is a romantic, first-class start to your new life together.

Just like weddings, honeymoons require careful planning. Thoroughly research your destination beforehand and make reservations in advance for any restaurants, spa treatments, or other activities that you would love to try. While there is something to be said for spontaneity, you also don't want to end up dining at a subpar restaurant because you were unable to get a table somewhere better. You don't need to schedule activities for every day of your trip, but it is always a good idea to build in a few romantic experiences.

Generally paid for by the groom and his family, the honeymoon is rarely factored into the overall wedding budget. You may, however, want to use the points you've accrued on your wedding credit card to purchase airline tickets or upgrade hotel suites. If you can afford the luxury, I recommend flying first class. You have just experienced the most memorable event of your life. For the past several weeks you've been in the spotlight and treated like royalty; continue the pampering throughout your trip.

JUST THE BEGINNING

The end of the wedding and honeymoon marks the beginning of the marriage. However, after the excitement of getting married, actual marriage can feel anticlimactic.

Never lose sight of the original reason behind the wedding. You exchange vows because you love each other and want to spend your lives together. Planning a wedding is stressful on a number of levels; it can bring out the worst sides of people. I too often see couples allow the planning process to strain their relationship. Stress affects the body in unexpected ways: headaches, achy muscles, frequent colds, mood swings, difficulty sleeping, stomachaches, loss of appetite, increase in appetite, feelings of isolation—the list goes on. It's not uncommon for perfectly healthy couples to experience one or more of these symptoms during the wedding-planning process. They're not sick, just stressed. Unfortunately, most of us take out our frustration on the people we love most. Shortly after you get engaged, have a frank discussion with your soon-to-be-spouse about how planning a wedding will affect your relationship in the short term. Devise a code word that can serve as a gentle reminder that the love you share for one another is far more important than the wedding itself. It's easy to get swept away in the details. Whether it's just the two of you or you're in a crowded room, saying this simple code word will offer a nonconfrontational reality check. After all, the ultimate goal is to be married, to love and support one another, and to be happier together than you are apart. The creation of a marriage is the motivation behind shopping for the perfect gown, hiring a florist, planning the menu, booking the venue, and all the other minute details that planning a wedding entails. Never place the event before your relationship.

My grandfather once gave me some great advice that I often share with my brides. I hope that it means something to you and helps you with your marriage as it has helped me with mine. "Beginnings are usually happy. Endings are usually sad. The only thing that really counts is what happens in the middle."

the post-honeymoon checklist

☐ Contact the following with your change of name. (You can purchase a name change kit to assist you with these details.)
- Social Security Administration
- United States Postal Office
- Department of Motor Vehicles for driver's license
- Passport office
- Human Resources Department of your employer
- Credit card companies
- Bank or credit union
- 401 K or retirement plans
- Voter registration
- Doctors
- Dentists
- Health insurance company
- Health, life, homeowner and auto insurance companies
- Mortgage company
- Clubs and memberships
- Frequent flyer cards
- Utility companies
- Attorney (any contracts you have in place as well as your will)

☐ Review your wedding photography and return the images you want in your albums.

☐ Review the first draft of your wedding video and return it to the videographer with any editing requests.

☐ Drop off your wedding gown for cleaning and preservation.

☐ Write and mail thank-you cards to your guests and wedding vendors.

☐ Return any borrowed items.

☐ Send an announcement and photograph to your local newspaper's wedding department.

☐ Entertain the close family and friends that helped you during the wedding-planning process. You could host a dinner party or take a few to dinner at a favorite restaurant. It is not necessary to thank them all at once, but you ought to gradually show them all how much you appreciate their support.

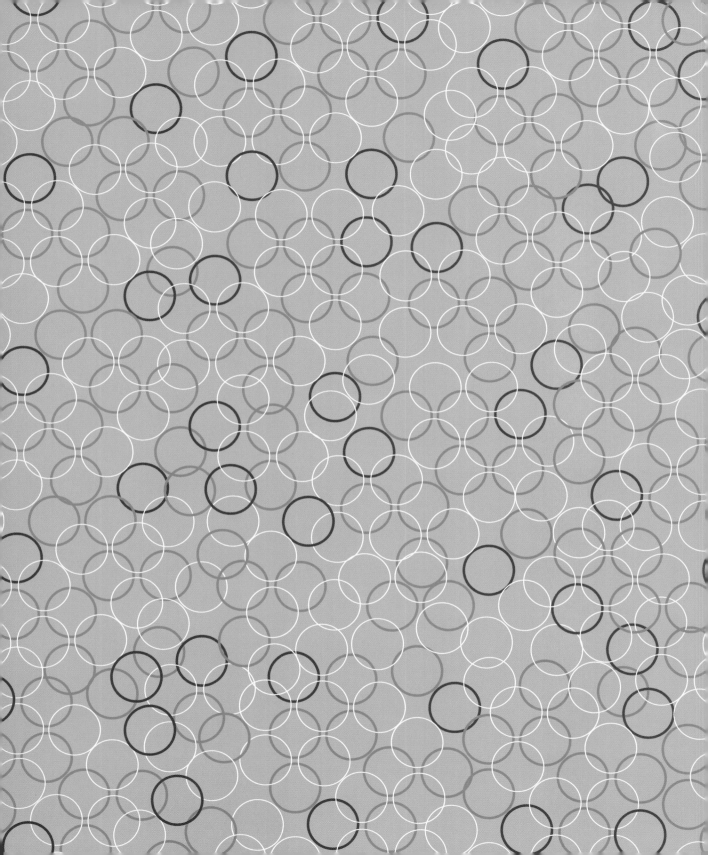

ACKNOWLEDGMENTS

visual image photography

I do so many weddings with Carmine and Hilary LiDestri that they were an easy choice when deciding on the photographer for this book. Their work is known all over Texas as being the best of the best. I am so grateful to them for helping me select the right images and making this book so much more beautiful with their amazingly creative eyes. (www.lidestriphoto.com)

hilary lidestri

Hilary has been the one who most challenges me to move forward. She continually motivates me to think outside the box and encourages me to sidestep the many hurdles that have gotten in my way. In many ways, especially literary, she is one of the most incredibly talented and creative people I know. Hilary was an invaluable resource as I was writing the photography chapter. She had some very useful input and was a great support system.

luana stoutmeyer

Luana is the person I often turn to when I need assistance regarding business decisions and ethical issues. She is an outstanding entertainment agent and has given so much to the wedding and event industry. Luana offered valuable advice and information for several sections in this book, particularly the entertainment chapter. (www.encoreproductions.ws)

lisa pulice-dalton

Lisa Dalton is an amazing addition to the wedding industry in Dallas. In fact, I have known her longer than I have known anyone else in the local industry. She is a pro when it comes to maintaining sanity while dealing with the rigors of the day-to-day event business. I turned to Lisa to share with me how she does it. Her wisdom is scattered throughout the book's sections on venue selection and catering. (www.hotelpalomar.com)

jenny cline and marsha ballard-french

Jenny and Marsha are known for their incredible Texas-based full-service wedding department store, Stardust Celebrations, which has been featured on both *Whose Wedding Is It Anyway?* and *Married Away*. Stardust is *the* destination for Texan brides and is where I take many of my clients gown shopping. They also have a large selection of stunning wedding accessories. Jenny and Marsha assisted me with the gown chapter of this book, and their advice was invaluable. (www.stardustcelebrations.com)

geni morin

A veteran catering manager and wedding professional, Geni brought to the table a great deal of insight. She is a wonderful personality and precious soul. I could not have gotten to this point without her in my inner circle. (www.creativecuisinegroup.com)

marcus rollins

Marcus is one of the most incredible disc jockey/masters of ceremonies I have ever met. He has a knack for adding personal elements to a wedding, and I always refer him when I have the chance. Marcus reviewed my entertainment chapter and offered some great input. (www.marcusrollins.com)

SPECIAL THANKS

my team

Matthew Lindley, my partner; Molly Rasmussen, my wonderful and lovely assistant planner without whom I could not have had the time to get this book done; Nena Madonia and Jan Miller, my incredible literary agents; Sarah Hall and her amazing publicity team—especially Ashley Lanaux, my publicity coordinator; James DeFrange for continually styling me young; Cindy Holub, one of my oldest friends in the world and the person who helped me to elevate my thinking from being a kid to a man; and Robbi Ernst III, my mentor.

my tv family

Executive producer Shawn Visco, senior producer Jason Fine, and the rest of the folks at True Entertainment; all the wonderful people at The Style Network; Loreen Stevens, my longtime casting guru; and Timothy Hedden, who produced many of my television shows.

the couples

Rene and Troy Sarria, Sanya Richards and Aaron Ross, Marlane and Donn Willins, Caitlin and Joe Cassin, Hilary and Carmine LiDestri, Shea and Lee Cochran, Dr. Christine Carman and Allen Stiles, Tiffany and Dale Wilson, Jennifer and Evan Shrago, Torei and Zibbora Crane, Ann Marie and Brendan Morrow, Margaret and Joey Pellicone, Amber and Greg Rand, Heather and Ryan Schamerloh, Laura and Shawn Zaramaksi, Lori and Caleb Medefind, Antonia and Ben Scotti, Kelle and Danny Schreiber, Mary Katherine and Dustin Elam, Kari and Aaron Boyd, Meredith and Joseph Behgooy, Lindsay and Brandan Harris—thank you so much for allowing me to feature photographs from your weddings.

other contributors

Romano's Bakery, Hotel Palomar, Cobin Kraddick, Functions Creative, Stardust Celebrations, Little Palm Island Resort, and Holly Tripp—thank you.

my family

I want to thank my parents, Sue and Sonny Brown, for all their encouragement and support. I always wanted to build a name for myself and make them proud. This has always been a driving force in my life and career, and I love them very much. A special thanks to my sister and her family, the Jasons—D'anna, Mark, Chris, Andrea, and Stephanie. Also, I am so happy to have my extended family: Meleda, Rod, Greg, Grandmom, and Kevin. People often dread their in-laws. I don't have that problem. They are wonderful people and have accepted me as a part of their family. I am a truly lucky man!

in memoriam

I want to mention my incredible grandparents, Estelle and AC Kirk. They laid the foundation for me to become the man I am today; teaching me what was right and what was wrong. I will always love and miss them.

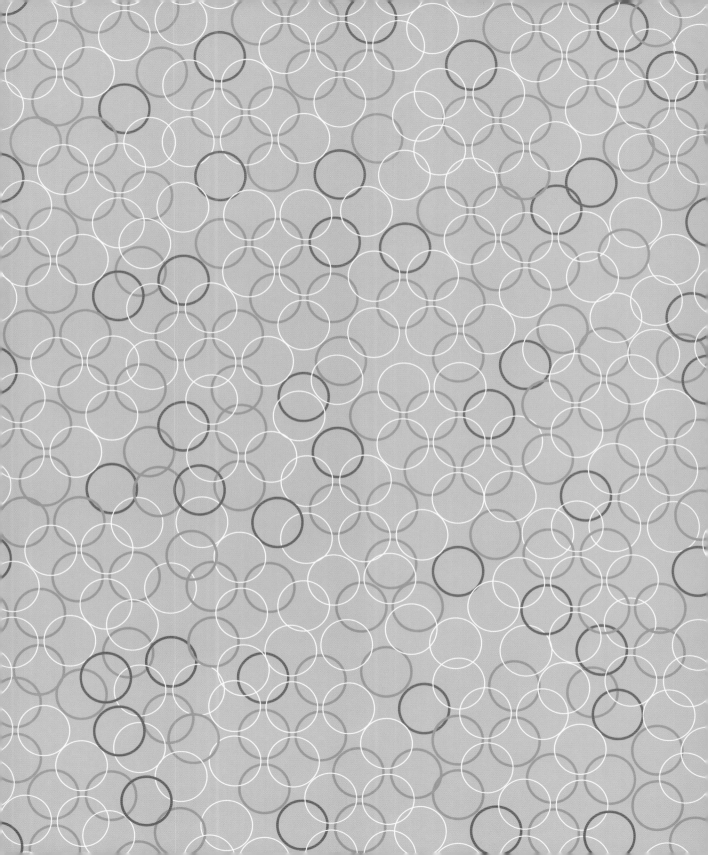

INDEX

Published in 2009 by Stewart, Tabori & Chang
An imprint of ABRAMS

Library of Congress Cataloging-in-Publication Data:
Brown, Donnie.
  Donnie Brown weddings : from the couture to the cake / by Donnie Brown.
      p. cm.
  Includes index.
  ISBN 978-1-58479-791-3
  1. Weddings—United States. 2. Weddings—United States—Planning. I. Title.
  HQ745.B863 2009
  395.2'2—dc22
2009007177

Editor: Ann Stratton
Designer: Jill Groeber
Production Manager: Tina Cameron

Stewart, Tabori & Chang books are available at special discounts when purchased in quantity
for premiums and promotions as well as fundraising or educational use. Special editions can also
be created to specification. For details, contact specialmarkets@hnabooks.com.

Printed and bound in China
10 9 8 7 6 5 4 3 2 1

THE ART OF BOOKS SINCE 1949
115 West 18th Street
New York, NY 10011
www.abramsbooks.com